As Christians we know that mor
often we default to this behaviou
want to change we don't always
guide gives a clear and simple fr
know we need to make. But chan
heart, and this book starts by h
lenging, mirror for us to assess w

actions. It is grounded in God's character and plans for his people and
shows how we can honour him with our time, money and priorities.
Jeremy Anderson, senior city finance professional

The Money Mentor is a gem of a little book with practical, common-sense
guidance on how to live within one's means, combined with solid biblical
insights about the roles that money and material possessions play in our
lives. It explains the constant attack on both our common sense and
Scripture's principles that we experience daily through advertisement
and the government, but gives us hope for ways to fight back and win
– at least at the level of our personal, our family's and our church's
finances. Strongly recommended!
Craig Blomberg, Distinguished Professor of New Testament, Denver Seminary

This is a book that needed writing! Practical help to consider money, its
godly place, and how the Christian should joyfully use it rather than
joining the world in being ruled by it! Writing for Christians, Ash has
given every one of us, rich or poor, new or mature believer, some fabulous
biblical and worldly-wise insights that will undoubtedly challenge and
help every reader.
*Richard Borgonon, who has combined a senior City of London career with
over twenty-five years of chairing Christian charities and leading church
finances*

A radical and challenging application of the Bible to a key issue for today.
David Jackman, former President of the Proclamation Trust

I warmly welcome the publication of this excellent little book, which I
wish had been written many years ago. It is filled with practical, down-
to-earth advice and is based on sound scriptural principles. Whether you
are starting out in life or have plenty of experience of managing your

finances, you will find things here to help you as well as to challenge your thinking and behaviour.

Simon Pilcher, Chief Executive, Fixed Income, M&G Investments and Director of M&G Ltd, is also a lay preacher and churchwarden

The Bible talks so much about money that it leaves us in no doubt as to its absolutely critical importance as an issue. In recent years the cost of having a wrong attitude to money and a lack of practical financial management skills have been shockingly apparent in our world, and unfortunately in many of our churches and Christian lives also, and that is why this book is so timely.

Faithfulness to the Bible's teaching on money and a radical heart to live it out from day to day give Christians a wonderful opportunity to live distinctive and truly rich lives, regardless of how materially rich or poor we may be. The clear, practical and faithful approach modelled in *The Money Mentor* makes it an absolutely terrific guide for anyone who wants to be challenged and inspired in equal measure to get godly with their money.

Chris Tapp, Director, Credit Action

I'm grateful to God and to Ash for this book. It's clear, very practical, extremely comprehensive (covering everything from world-views to wills) and steeped in the Scriptures. But what really excited me about it is how Ash shows us the connections between the mundane (and at times dull) realities of money management and our radical love for our King who died for us and is coming again. Whether you think you're 'sorted' financially, just about in control of things or in a total mess, this book is a great spur for us all to consider how Christians can honour Jesus with their cash.

John Taylor, student worker, City Church, Birmingham

This book is based on and shaped by a thorough theological grasp of God's grace. It provides outstanding practical advice on how Christians should handle their finances. There is little else like it. It will be widely appreciated by church leaders and members alike. Highly recommended!

Revd William Taylor, Rector of St Helen's Church, Bishopsgate, London

Ash Carter

The Money Mentor

Getting to grips with your finances

ivp

For downloadable resources,
please visit ivpbooks.com/resources

INTER-VARSITY PRESS
Norton Street, Nottingham NG7 3HR, England
Email: ivp@ivpbooks.com
Website: www.ivpbooks.com

First published 2010

British Library Cataloguing in Publication Data
A catalogue record for this book is available from the British Library.

ISBN: 978-1-84474-490-9

Set in Dante 12/15pt
Typeset in Great Britain by CRB Associates, Potterhanworth, Lincolnshire
Printed and bound in Great Britain by Ashford Colour Press Ltd, Gosport,
Hampshire

Inter-Varsity Press publishes Christian books that are true to the Bible and
that communicate the gospel, develop discipleship and strengthen the church
for its mission in the world.

Inter-Varsity Press is closely linked with the Universities and Colleges
Christian Fellowship, a student movement connecting Christian Unions
in universities and colleges throughout Great Britain, and a member
movement of the International Fellowship of Evangelical Students.
Website: www.uccf.org.uk

For Mim,
my wife, my love, my co-worker in Christ,
and for my boys, Harry and Tim.
May you grow up to love Jesus more than your parents.

CONTENTS

ACKNOWLEDGMENTS

I am conscious as I write this that I am bound to leave someone out from the list below. And even if you're mentioned, getting your name in print can scarcely be thanks enough. For the contributions made by so many, I am in your debt, one and all.

I am profoundly thankful to all those who have taught me to understand and to obey God's word. There's a long way still to go, but thanks for your fellowship on the journey so far.

My thanks in general go to the staff team at St Helen's, Bishopsgate. I could not have hoped to be in a happier place over the past four years. I spent most of that time wondering how on earth I had been given such a privilege. Our God is so gracious. Thank you, too, for opportunities to present this material in various contexts – it has sharpened it no end.

My especial thanks are due to Michael and Leonie and all my peers on the Associate Scheme, in whose company some of these ideas took more solid form. Keep up the good work, one and all.

For the fact that this book ever became anything more than a private project, I am grateful to Iain Drummond and Andrew Sach. Thank you for your encouragements and for suggesting that I get in touch with IVP about it.

My thanks too must go to my friends Rich Alldritt, David Dargue and Dave Puttick, whose reading of the manuscript and helpful comments made it a better book than it otherwise would have been. Your friendship, insight and godliness are an inspiration to me far beyond this book.

I am also grateful to Charlie and Judith for their wisdom on pocket money for grown-ups. Truly a marriage-saver!

I ought to thank my English teacher, Mrs M., without whose encouragement I might never have become an accountant . . .

I reserve special thanks for my editor at IVP, Eleanor Trotter, who has taken up this project with gusto from the day my first draft landed on her desk. Her grace and patience have helped this novice through the painful process of committing a book to paper, and for that I am truly grateful. Her work, and that of all the team at IVP, has made this book infinitely better than it might have been. Any errors that remain are, of course, entirely mine.

To my wife, Mim, go all thanks always. God knew exactly whom I needed to help me grow in Christ, and I am thankful for you in so many ways. Thank you for supporting this book, for reading early drafts, and for picking up the pieces at home when the book distracted me from the business of living from day to day.

To my elder son, Harry, who has lived with this manuscript for most of his life: I'm sorry that Daddy was sometimes a bit *too* distracted. Shall we go and play with your cars now?

Finally, and always, to my Lord and Saviour, Jesus Christ: thank you for opening my eyes to see something of your glory. Please help me to obey all that you have shown me.

INTRODUCTION

Jesus called his church 'the light of the world'. Of it he said, 'A city set on a hill cannot be hidden.'[1] I wonder if we feel like light. Does your church or mine seem like a shining lamp, a place of great godliness and love, a place of peace ruled by God's word and radiating his love to a world in darkness?

We shouldn't underestimate the effect that a loving community of Christians can have on the world. Nevertheless, when I read words like those above I have to confess to feeling like a 40-watt bulb when I ought to be a lighthouse lamp.

Perhaps one reason why we do not shine as brightly as we ought to is that in many areas the world is encroaching upon *us*. The world holds out its ambitions, its gods, its way of life, and we are drawn to them like moths to a flame.

In every generation, it is the role of the church to assess how we can live in God's world while waiting for the next, and to live in a radical way that shows the hope we have in our Saviour, Jesus Christ, and the way such hope changes us today. This applies as much to money as to any area of Christian living.

Where you're at
Perhaps you have picked up this book because you are in real financial distress. If that is the case, I hope that it will be immensely helpful to you in sorting out your difficult situation

and in saving you from many future pitfalls. But I also hope that, whether you are in trouble or not, it will help you to live to please God in the way that you handle money.

You may be one of many readers who have picked up this book, a little concerned that it might have nothing to say to you. Life may be comfortable and you don't need a book on money to help you out. Nevertheless, there is a far deeper question that this book also seeks to address.

God's angle

The most important question we can ask on the subject of money is not, 'How can I get out of this mess?' Rather, we must ask, 'How can I honour God with all that he has given me?' That question applies to all of life, but it is especially relevant to the area of money.

Before looking at what we can do to bring our money under control, we'll need to think through what the Bible says about it. We will need to understand what faithful stewardship looks like, so that, when we come to practical wisdom, we apply it in the right way.

In order to do this, we are going to explore some important theological foundations. Let me give you four gospel reasons and one practical reason why not to skip over them. First, no amount of practical wisdom will help if you cannot see *why* that wisdom is wise. Secondly, we cannot change for the longer term unless the change is motivated by the gospel. Change needs to happen at the level of our understanding of God and ourselves in his world, and not just in the practical details. Thirdly, the theological foundations will help us to see how money fits into God's big plan, so that we can make properly wise decisions. Fourthly, having the theological view will enable us to ask the right questions. This may not mean the ones that are most pressing for us at that moment, but perhaps the ones we most need to ask. Finally, I have meshed the theological material and the practical advice together so that it is not that easy to read one aspect without the other.

As part of all this, we will ask the following: who has the right to decide what I do with my money? If I am as sinful as the Bible says I am, can I trust my own heart not to deceive me? What would God have me live for? What does it look like to follow Jesus wholeheartedly while waiting for him to come back?

These and other questions will help us to discern a set of biblical priorities around which we can structure our practice.

But it is one thing to ask 'What does the Bible say?' and quite another to do what we are told. We'll take a step-by-step look at how to control our finances, including planning and taking practical measures to make that plan work, and how to keep good records. It is worth mentioning that, although I am writing from a UK context and giving illustrations in £ sterling, readers outside the UK will find that their situations are similar, even if some terms are different.

God wants us to honour him in the day-to-day decisions that cumulatively make up a life lived for him. My aim is to help every reader to love the Lord our God with all their heart, mind, soul and strength in the area of money.

Imagine . . .
Before we get there, let me set out a vision for our money management that might help us.

Imagine a church with no money worries because of the routine generosity of all who belong to it; where every member looks after every other member, so that nobody lacks any necessity of life. Imagine a global church free from poverty and the burden of excess wealth because of generosity between congregations.

Imagine Christians making decisions about their career based on what is best for their family and church, and not on what will get them more money and a better job.

Imagine a church full of people making decisions to serve God in numerous ways that don't get noticed by anyone but the one audience that matters.

Imagine a church in which many of our current financial problems don't exist because we've chosen to live God's way, within our means and by being generous (and receiving generosity from others). Imagine a church in which every Christian is trying to live out biblical wisdom in this fundamental area.

Imagine a church that stands out from a materialistic culture by living distinctively God's way.

Imagine . . .

Ash Carter
July 2010

CHAPTER 1

WHERE IT ALL STARTED AND HOW IT ALL WENT WRONG

Before considering how we ought to think about money, I'd like to ask you a very direct question: what is your default position? We are all raised in a particular culture where there is an underlying way of thinking and a set of influences of which we are often not aware.

Where it all started

First of all, let's step back and focus on some financial and social trends from the past few decades. Space forbids me from being comprehensive here, but I do want to survey some of the developments that have brought us to the place where we now are.

Richer than ever

It may seem like a crazy thing to say, given that we are more in debt than we have ever been, but we are also richer than any previous generation.

According to the Office of National Statistics (ONS), between 1971 and 2002 there was a rise in disposable income (income left over after paying for essentials, such as food) of about 75% if you were on a fairly average income.[1] This was after adjusting the 1971 figures to account for today's prices.

Other evidence from the ONS[2] suggests that the cost of essentials has also risen. What this means is that we earn more money than in 1971 and we spend more on essentials now, presumably because of the variety of options available in the supermarkets. And *still* we have more disposable income than we had four decades ago.

Which should mean that we are in less debt than ever before, but . . .

Everyone wants to get their mitts on your money

You see, every company in the world wants to get their hands on that disposable income. And they want to do it in the most profitable way possible.

For example, as we've seen, the range of goods available in your supermarket has increased dramatically in the past forty years, and one reason for this is that we are now richer. And since we are richer, we can shop for wants as well as needs. We can buy the fairtrade bananas, the exotic coffees and the bizarre fruits we have never heard of. We can buy a larger basket of goods, of wants as well as essentials, and the supermarkets can make more money.

Whole industries have sprung up to serve our wealthier generation: industries in recreation, in long-haul holidays, in clothing and technologies. Many provide for our needs, but a great deal of time is spent serving our wants too.

The UK advertising industry is worth £400 billion[3] per year, and that figure keeps rising. A great deal of advertising is designed to persuade us that our wants are really needs, and that those needs can be best satisfied by a certain brand of shampoo or wristwatch or car. 'Advertising thrives on instilling discontent'[4] and then offering contentment through the latest toys.

So we have more money to spend than any previous generation, and a great deal is spent by others in persuading us to part with it, persuading us to want products so badly that we will spend what we don't even have in order to buy them.

But, even if you *want* to spend more money than you actually have, you can't do so unless someone is willing to lend it to you. Which brings us neatly to . . .

The rise . . . and rise of credit

Just imagine this situation: if I wanted to, I could buy a house with a 100% mortgage. I could buy a car to go in the driveway, also on credit. I could buy furniture to go in the house on four years' interest-free credit. Then I could buy clothes and all the technological gadgets I could ever want on the many credit cards I have been offered. Or at least I could have done that until the credit bubble burst. Yet even now, with lenders being more cautious about what they lend and to whom, are we as borrowers starting to change our habits? Certainly we are still credit-hungry.

In generations past you simply didn't spend what you hadn't already earned; indeed, you couldn't have done so. According to Keith Tondeur, 'Since 1983 the amount of money owing in Britain on mortgages, credit and store cards has multiplied twenty times.'[5] Historically, it was simply impossible to spend money that hadn't been given to you first, so the transformation in the past three decades has been quite alarming. You can acquire credit on almost everything, as though every sports club, high-street shop and airline in the world were also a bank. You can have so much access to credit that it is sometimes hard to remember that *at some point* everything needs to be paid for.

On top of that, statistics show that people spend one-third more when buying on credit rather than with cash, because they do not feel that they are actually spending money![6] We are just deceiving ourselves. The credit crunch may have changed the availability of credit, at least for a time, but until *we* change, the same dangers will be lurking there for us that have been lurking for decades.

The boundaries that used to be set by what we earned have become endlessly fluid. We can spend far beyond our means and far more quickly than we can earn. Our wants have become needs, and are being married beautifully to our increased capacity to buy those wanted items. Even though the truth is that we are spending someone else's money.

A relative of mine who works for a global bank told me that some of their internal research showed that people tend to spend to the limit on their credit cards. Then they come to the bank and ask for a loan to clear the credit card. The bank often extends their credit limit because they are 'a good customer' (this happened to me too), and the individual spends to the credit-card limit once again.

Providing the cardholder makes the required payments, eventually, then the banks are fine. Banks make much more money from credit cards than on mortgages because the rates of interest are so much higher. It is easy money, and they know we can afford it because, after all, we are richer than ever before.

I hope that you are beginning to see the picture here. We have much more money passing through our hands than any previous generation, some of it ours and some lent by others. At the same time, the whole economy rests on getting us to part with it. And that is why you have . . .

The problem with politics

Every organization has an aim, a reason why it exists. For a company, that aim is to further the interests of the shareholders in the business. For most businesses, that will involve making money for the owners. The owners tell the board of directors their aims, and the directors are expected to do what they are told.

The directors know that their job depends on meeting those aims, so they run the business accordingly.

The same thing is true for the government. We are shareholders with a stake in the proper running of the country we live in. Everyone wants the government to do them good. Put it all together, and a wise government will try to please as many people as it possibly can.

Now, suppose there was a clash between what was *actually* best for the majority in the country and what the majority *thought* was best. What should the government do then?

Take war, for example. Suppose that a government could see the need for war, but nobody else could. Should they go to war because they are elected to do what is best for the country? Or should they do what the majority think is best in order to preserve their own jobs?

The problem of old age

Let's take a real-life example. As a population, we are getting progressively older: the retired live longer and there are fewer children being born each year.[7] In the longer term, what that means is that there are fewer people working and earning money to pay the government in taxes to pay out to retired people in the form of pensions. So let's say, for argument's sake, that there is a pension crisis brewing. What do you do?

The answer is pretty straightforward. The government ought to persuade everyone to save. The problem is that this will not be very popular. If every working person in the country saved £1,000 this year for their pension, then that would pull £30 billion out of the economy[8] as we invest for our retirement. That means pulling £30 billion of retail sales on wants out of the economy.

That means job losses, businesses going bust. It means pulling a lot of taxes out of the economy too.

Imagine if everyone decided to pay off their unsecured debts this year too. That would pull another £150 billion out of the economy, money that cannot be paid in wages to be re-spent and re-spent. The total cost to the economy could run to over £300 billion.

And this is the problem for the government. In the long term, we desperately need healthy private savings and pension provisions that will look after us into a long retirement, but they will come at the short-term cost of jobs and, significantly, government popularity.

So the government will always decide to do what the majority of the populace think is best, even if the longer-term consequences are disastrous. After all, they won't be in power when we get to the distant future.

The government is not helped in this situation by a series of factors. Our credit culture means that we are not used to thinking long-term when it comes to money, and, at the same time, the deteriorating standards of basic numeracy in schools mean that many people leave formal education unable to think through such basic issues as the percentage rates on debt.

In short, the government is not in a position to help us deal with our financial struggles because truly helping us would be political suicide.

The problem is me

I wonder how you are feeling right now. It is quite easy to read an analysis like that, isn't it? If the person to blame is out there, some faceless character to be booed at like a pantomime villain, then we can all rest comfortably in our bad habits and nothing needs to change.

We have no positive influences on us financially. We have a government that cannot intervene in a culture that wants everything now. We have been soaked in advertising for so long and had the hand of credit extended to us so often that we have begun to think it is normal.

But it isn't. We have got this badly wrong, and for the sake of the church we need to get God's house in order. I'm going to focus on our self-deception, but everything I will say applies to the church more generally too. We are afraid to talk about money. We don't model good stewardship, and too often we openly model *bad* stewardship of God's resources.

In Proverbs 1:8–9 we read:

Hear, my son, your father's instruction,
   and forsake not your mother's teaching,
for they are a graceful garland for your head
   and pendants for your neck.

Solomon wants us to take the wise advice of our fathers because it will keep us safe from folly. But, when it comes to money, the church and the home have often been bereft of wise advice. My hope is that this book will provoke us to wiser living and godly community. Whatever your financial story, now is the time for change.

But the advert said . . .

The truth is that, whatever your financial situation, you got there because you wanted to get there. Ouch! That sounds a bit harsh, doesn't it? But it is true. I got into debt because I was reckless and undisciplined.

The truth is that I believed the adverts. The *real* truth is that I *wanted* to believe the adverts. I wanted the bright and shiny Hollywood life, where it was always sunny and everything was beautifully plastic. OK, that isn't exactly my idea of a fantasy world, but I have bought into the adverts and so too have you. We've all spent money we shouldn't have spent on things we didn't need. For most of us, this is such a habit that we don't even notice it any more.

Life can feel humdrum, difficult even. So when the advert promises us a new life, we really want it to be true. It's so much easier to change your life by buying *that* car or wristwatch. Much easier than following Jesus, certainly. And that is where it bites for us as Christians. Jesus has promised us the only world where everything will be perfect all the time, where everyone will be truly beautiful, and where everything we experience will always be a delight.

But it is just so hard following Jesus. It would be great to be able to have it all *now*. Clearly, if it were a straight choice between having it now or having it in heaven, then we'd take heaven every time. But we can chase both, right? We can have the picture-perfect life here and get the sports version in heaven too?

A heart problem?

Jeremiah 17:9 tells us that 'the heart is deceitful above all things and beyond cure. Who can understand it?' (NIV).

That is to say, we have a spiritual problem, an active self-deception from the very core of us. What is the nature of that self-deception?

In Jeremiah it is idolatry. God's people worshipped every god in creation but not the Creator himself. That is our heart too, every one of us. From Genesis 3 onwards, every one of us has preferred to look for our soul's satisfaction in anything other than God. At every point in history, human beings have looked to their harvests, their families, their trinkets and their toys to fill the deep longing in their hearts that can be filled only by a relationship with God.

That is why advertising works. We all function in the same way. We are sinful, and the advertisers play on our lust for created things, feeding our desire and then feeding *from* it. I don't mean to make the advertisers out to be more demonic than the rest of us. It is just that they are *like* us, and they know exactly what makes us all tick.

That is why we are so complicit in the mess we are in. When the advertiser tells us that we will be much more attractive with *that* car or *those* shoes, and we nod and say, 'Yes, I really would', then we are buying into a lie. We are prepared to believe, *want* to believe, that we can find real happiness apart from God. And so we will listen to anyone who offers us that chance, however stupid it may be.

We are sinful. Our hearts are in rebellion against God. Not only mine and yours, but everyone else's too. So we have a whole economy that is built on the universal idolatries of the age. Money, power, sex and health are all used to sell us things that promise so much but cannot deliver what God alone can give us: happiness.

When I chase that job, that car or whatever else, when I tell myself that I can have it now *and* in God's future, I am actually rejecting God and choosing the creation *over* the Creator.

Fighting back

As I began to get my head around all this, I began to realize that I can't somehow run in neutral. I can't *know* all this and not *do* something about it. If I don't change, if my habits don't change, then I will keep being sucked in by a system that wants my money in exchange for tat that I don't need. Worse still, I will abandon God in the hopeless pursuit of empty promises.

I needed to change.

I am guessing that you do too. That is why I am writing this book. I won't claim that I have sorted this out for myself. As with every area of godliness, this is something I will need to work at my whole life long. But I want to start us off on a journey in the right direction.

We all have a choice. We can live in this world as Jesus did, for his Father's honour and for the salvation of others. Or we can live, as most in our society do, as if Jesus had never been born. What we choose matters profoundly.

We can live in this world as Jesus did, for his Father's honour and for the salvation of others. Or we can live, as most in our society do, as if Jesus had never been born.

The apostle Paul tells us that the aim of his ministry is to present everyone mature in Christ on the final day (Colossians 1:28). What does that mean? In Ephesians 4 we are told that a mature church is one that is able to withstand every false ideology. Maturing happens as we, the church, speak the truth to one another in love. This truth is not just the cross, but a whole view of God, his universe, humanity and the purpose of life, in which Jesus is the centre. What we need is a whole new world-view.

Battle of the world-views

What Paul is talking about in the New Testament is what philosophers call a world-view. James W. Sire has defined it like this:

> **A worldview is a commitment, a fundamental orientation of the heart, that can be expressed as a story or in a set of presuppositions (assumptions which may be true, partially true or entirely false) which we hold (consciously or subconsciously, consistently or**

inconsistently) about the basic constitution of reality, and that provides the foundation on which we live and move and have our being.[9]

What Sire is basically saying is that your world-view is what you believe about what defines reality. Does God exist? What is he like? Are people basically good or evil? Is there such a thing as right and wrong, and who says which is which?

These are the sorts of question Sire poses. The answers form your basic view of reality. And your view of reality is the foundation for the whole of your life. It works a bit like this: my views on right and wrong, for example, form my views of what it is good to do, which in turn shape my likes and dislikes, which control my lifestyle choices.

We all have a world-view. The key question is: is your world-view true?

As a Christian, I believe that God has revealed to us the core truths that should form our world-view. I also believe that everything and everyone around us is trying to persuade us of a different world-view.

When the advertiser tells me that I can have the truly satisfied life with *that* aftershave, he is offering to play God and give me the future that only God can provide. He is presenting a totally different world-view.

It might be fairer to say that we all have two world-views. The battle that Paul encounters in Romans 7, between his fleshly, worldly self and the Spirit-filled, regenerate, transformed self, is what you might call the battle of the world-views. It is the battle of two views of reality competing for control of the Christian's life.

I will make a number of claims for God in this book. But we need to be persuaded that God is absolutely right if we are really going to change. If we do not believe that God has spoken definitively in the Bible, then our hearts will always persuade us to find a different path from that which he commands. Paul's deep conviction of the truth of the Bible is why he preaches Christ to make people mature, and why the church builds itself up in love as we speak the truth to one another.

At every stage we need to encourage one another away from lies to the reality about Jesus and a right view of the world and the God who made it, so that we can make wise and godly decisions.

We have been given a set of values by the world around us, but we are going to need to hold our own lives up to the mirror of Scripture and ask ourselves how much needs to change.

We can change

It is one thing to want to change; it is quite another to do it.

It is no good simply adding Christian behaviour on to the way the world thinks, the way that *we* think. All that will do is make us feel guilty and miserable, and make us into Pharisees (hypocrites) too.

And we need not just a change in action but a complete change of direction. We need to ask God to act to change our desires and our deepest beliefs, so that when our hearts try to deceive us we have something deeper still that cries out, 'There is a better way.' We need to tear down the idols that we have willingly erected in our hearts and come back to God alone and let him fulfil our deepest longings.

Imagine that someone you have never met was watching your life, looking at your bank statements, seeing everything you did with your money. What would your priorities for your money say about what was really important to you?

The church must 'demonstrate to the watching world how different is the attitude of redeemed people toward the wealth that cannot survive the end of this age'.[10]

So just pause here and think of all the things you would love to see your church involved in, missionaries you would love to support. Think of the opportunities that are lost every time we make a worldly choice with God's money.

We need to change, and the gospel can change us. We're going to see how.

CHAPTER 2

WHO WANTS TO LIVE FOREVER?[1]

Meet John. He is thirty-six years old and works the night shift at the local industrial laundrette. John is trying to support his wife and three kids on £15,000 per year. He doesn't worry about the future because the present has enough worries of its own. Every month it is a struggle to pay the bills, and trying to keep the stress of it from the family is driving him to distraction. He is worried that he is failing as a parent and is too embarrassed to talk to anyone about it. You are the only person he is willing to talk to. What would you say to John?

Meet Charlie. She is twenty-six years old and on the graduate training programme of a major financial institution. She is single and enjoying it. She earns £65,000 per year before bonuses and she doesn't worry about the future either. In fact, her only current worry is how to keep up with her colleagues' lifestyle choices. Charlie is a Christian and she is susceptible to the temptation to live like her peers. Nevertheless, she's got a soft spot for clothes shopping, and as she can afford it, why not? What would you say to Charlie?

The above characters may be fictional, but the situations definitely aren't. As we saw in chapter 1, much of Western culture is about now – about gaining everything you want as soon as is decently possible. We might separate this into two ideas: what we want and when we want it.

What do we want?

What do people really want? You might get any number of answers to that question. One person might say that he wants to achieve something, to have a meaningful life. Another might say that she wants to be fulfilled, to reach her true potential. Another might wish to live a long, peaceful and secure life with his family. We all want to be happy. All the answers are really just different routes that an individual might choose to reach the goal of happiness.

When do we want it?

The answer to that one is pretty easy, isn't it? Everyone wants to be happy now. The future is uncertain, and if there are no guarantees that I will live long enough to have my happiness in my old age, I had better have it now.

You can see this in the dominant philosophies of our age as well. Secular humanism says that we are all evolving to perfection, so we should follow our heart's desires. There is no right or wrong, no morality; there are just good and bad experiences. So just do what makes you happy.

Scientific materialism says that this world is all there is, so whatever you are looking to for happiness, it had better be tangible. If you can't taste, smell or see it, then it probably doesn't exist.

Under society's skin

What humanism and materialism have in common is that they

both deny the existence and activity of God in the world. So God can't make promises. But the God of the Bible *does* make promises, and what he promises is a perfect future with him in the new creation. Throughout history, believing God's promises of a certain, perfect future has enabled Christians to live differently, to face persecution and suffering even, but without losing hope.

Our society says that God doesn't exist. That means there is no certainty about the future; there are no promises to believe in. And that means we had better get our happiness *now*.

Every world-view or philosophy, in the end, wants what God has promised, but without having to believe in him. They seek the blessings God promises by means of created things, and those things become their gods. Perhaps it is money, career, fame, sex or relationships. All of these are good in their proper place. But when they are asked to do God's job, they become idols.

Money can't purchase happiness

As Christians, we can buy into the above philosophy just as much as everyone else. Both John and Charlie, in their own ways, are looking for a better life now because they have forgotten that God has promised them real lasting happiness in the future.

I will go so far as to say that nothing, apart from God, will be able to bring us enduring happiness. The Old Testament book of Ecclesiastes makes that point well. The writer conjures up King Solomon for us, a king who had everything he could possibly want. And Solomon went looking for his soul's satisfaction in pleasure, in work, in wisdom. He was the master of all he surveyed, building stately homes and landscaped gardens and putting together his own choirs, just for pleasure. In the end, though, our writer had to conclude that 'all was vanity and a striving after wind, and there was nothing to be gained under the sun' (Ecclesiastes 2:11).

In fact, living under the sun is the very thing that prevents us from finding our soul's satisfaction here. Our writer observes that the wise man and the fool die just the same (Ecclesiastes 2:16), and both die just like the beasts (Ecclesiastes 3:19). Death is the reason that no happiness can endure. It will take loved ones from you, and in the end it will take everything you have from you. It's not that art, music, romance or work are wrong, but they just don't endure.

So, says our writer, the pursuit of your soul's satisfaction here and now is doomed to failure.

John D. Rockefeller was an American oil baron and philanthropist of the late nineteenth and early twentieth century. It is rumoured that he was once asked what seemed a fair question for one of the world's wealthiest men: 'How much money is enough money?' Rockefeller replied, 'Always just a little bit more.'[2]

> *If it isn't God, then it cannot do what God does.*

Rockefeller understood what Ecclesiastes 5:10 says: 'He who loves money will not be satisfied with money, nor he who loves wealth with his income.' Money is not God. To ask money to satisfy your soul is to ask it to do something that it was never created for. The man who pursues wealth is always going to be disappointed, no matter how much he has.

This point can be applied to every god that we might set up. If it isn't God, then it cannot do what God does.

After Rockefeller died, his accountant was asked how much he had left behind. In one word, the accountant summed up the shame of seeking satisfaction in wealth: 'Everything.' Wealth is a blessing, but in the end it will leave you or you will leave it. Rockefeller knew that and he put his wealth to good use. Can we do the same?

So how can we ever be happy?

Have you ever watched a romantic film, one where the credits roll as the couple finally get together? At that moment everything seems right with the world, but have you ever asked, 'What happened next?' The film wants to tell you that finding the right person makes all of life rose-tinted and ecstatic. And we'd like to believe it too.

But if we were being cynical, we would know that ten minutes after the credits rolled the couple would have fallen out about something trivial, and the spell would have been broken. That is why the film stopped when it did. We go to the movies for fantasy, not to see daily reality played out on the screen.

So is it not possible to be happy in this life? Of course it is. But is it possible to experience permanent, lasting happiness? No, it isn't. In a fallen world, even the greatest joys come to an end, and all of life itself comes to an end. This is one of the reasons why death is so hard to deal with. We instinctively know that it is an interloper in God's creation and it makes all that we can achieve meaningless.

What we need, then, is to be able to get beyond this world to a place where the corruptions of this creation don't exist. When you read the last two chapters of Revelation, the last book of the Bible, you will find just such a place. The new creation that God brings in at the close of time is the place we were made for, the place our souls long for, because it alone is the place of perfect, enduring happiness.

Gaining the whole world

That is what Jesus means in Mark 8:36–38 when he says:

> **For what does it profit a man to gain the whole world and forfeit his life? For what can a man give in return for his life? For whoever is ashamed of me and of my**

**words in this adulterous and sinful generation, of him
will the Son of Man also be ashamed when he comes in
the glory of his Father with the holy angels.**

Imagine, says Jesus, being on your deathbed. You own the
whole world, you've got the best qualifications from the best
universities, and you are loved and adored by everyone. But you
are about to die. As you are about to leave everything you have
behind, it is painfully obvious that being with Jesus in eternity
was the only thing worth pursuing in this life.

We all want to be happy. But even if you had everything that
you thought would make you happy in this life, it would all be
taken from you in the end. And you would realize what folly it
had been to chase things that don't last and, in doing so, forfeit
the one thing you have that will last into eternity: your soul,
your very self.

The whole Bible story is moving towards the new creation.
And since the Bible is a God's-eye view of all that is important
in human history, it is the direction in which *everything* is
heading. And the question for all of us is this: given that this
is what God is about, are we prepared to make it what we are
about as well?

Bible principle 1:
Live for the new creation

God is going to replace this world, broken as it is by sin, with a
perfect new world in which we can enjoy his presence for all
eternity.

Living for the new creation means having a certain hope that
governs every choice we make. What jobs we do, whom we
spend our time with, whom we marry, what we do with our

money – all these life decisions will be controlled, to some extent, by whether or not we have our eyes fixed on the future. 'We should live differently because we see differently,' says Randy Alcorn.[3]

The prosperity (false) gospel

We should live differently because we know that our blessing is in the future. The tragedy is that many churches legitimize living for wealth and happiness today by teaching that you can have health and wealth (the blessings of the new creation) now, if only you have enough faith.

Even a cursory reading of the New Testament shows us that this has to be false. Every New Testament writer expects us to suffer now, following in Christ's footsteps, before we can experience his glory in our resurrection. The prosperity gospel tells us that God wants us to be rich now, when the Bible tells us now 'to share in his cross – in the next life we will share in his crown'.[4]

We are to take up our cross, not our crown, to follow Jesus (Mark 8:34; cf. Matthew 10:38). Indeed, suffering is a mark of true discipleship (Romans 8:17; 2 Timothy 3:12), and we should rightly be wary of becoming too comfortable in this life.

My fear for much of the Western church is that we acknowledge that this is theologically correct, but deny it in practice. The Bible says plainly that the path to future glory is cross-shaped, and yet in practice we accumulate possessions and experiences that make our lives comfortable here. Is it possible that our habits with money show that we don't really believe in living a cross-shaped life?

A present governed by the future

Alcorn says, 'We were made for only one person and one place. Jesus is the person and heaven is the place. Our purpose should pervade our approach to money.'[5]

Much of contemporary thinking about the new creation portrays it as harps, fluffy clouds and chamber music. If that is what you imagine, then it must be very hard to long for it. But the new creation is a physical place with all the joys of this world and none of the suffering, where we can enjoy our relationship with God unsullied for ever. It's a place to long for.

Paul is in a Roman jail (Philippians 1:7) and facing the possibility of death. Yet he refuses to feel sorry for himself. Although he is in chains, he is determined to keep striving for the new creation (Philippians 3:12–14). Paul rejoices that his imprisonment has given him the chance to tell the whole Roman guard the gospel. He is in chains, but the gospel is not.

At the end of the letter, Paul makes the following statement:

Not that I am speaking of being in need, for I have learned in whatever situation I am to be content. I know how to be brought low, and I know how to abound. In any and every circumstance, I have learned the secret of facing plenty and hunger, abundance and need. I can do all things through him who strengthens me. (Philippians 4:11–13)

What really matters

So how will this affect our attitudes? Let us begin with our attitude to ourselves. Paul forgets the past and is single-minded about going to be with Jesus. He considers his privileges and status to be irrelevant (Philippians 3:7–9). This doesn't mean that he throws his certificates and training into the bin. Indeed, in places Paul makes great use of his privileges to preserve his life (e.g. Acts 22:26–28). But whatever Paul has on earth doesn't matter, *mustn't* matter. If he were to value this life too highly, he might become distracted from the prize that God has offered him.

Paul's aim in life is to make it safely to the next, and he will forego anything in this life to get there. He then calls on all Christians to do the same (Philippians 3:17).

This doesn't mean that we don't value ourselves, but rather we value our souls sufficiently highly that we want to be with Jesus in paradise. Here's one place where I think this should make an impact: in our wants and needs.

Wants and needs
In the Sermon on the Mount, Jesus teaches on God's provision for his people. Note what God promises to do and what he calls us to do:

> Therefore I tell you, do not be anxious about your life, what you will eat or what you will drink, nor about your body, what you will put on. Is not life more than food, and the body more than clothing? Look at the birds of the air: they neither sow nor reap nor gather into barns, and yet your heavenly Father feeds them. Are you not of more value than they? And which of you by being anxious can add a single hour to his span of life? And why are you anxious about clothing? Consider the lilies of the field, how they grow: they neither toil nor spin, yet I tell you, even Solomon in all his glory was not arrayed like one of these. But if God so clothes the grass of the field, which today is alive and tomorrow is thrown into the oven, will he not much more clothe you, O you of little faith? Therefore do not be anxious, saying, 'What shall we eat?' or 'What shall we drink?' or 'What shall we wear?' For the Gentiles seek after all these things, and your heavenly Father knows that you need them all. But seek first the kingdom of God and his

righteousness, and all these things will be added to you. (Matthew 6:25–33)

Jesus commands us to seek first God's kingdom. We wait for Jesus to return, and in the meantime we seek to build his kingdom. This brings us back to the place we have been all along – living now as we wait for the new creation, the kingdom of King Jesus.

And we can do that without worrying (verses 25, 31) because God will provide all that we need. We don't need to worry about clothing or feeding ourselves, only about the kingdom of God.

Of course, God providing all that we *need* is not the same as providing all that we might *want*. In many ways, that is the challenge of this chapter. Are we willing to be content just with what we need, knowing that our future with Jesus in glory is guaranteed? Are we willing to trust God to provide? Or is our God too small to fulfil his promises?

The unbeliever chases after these things because he has no hope in God. He wants his blessings now, wants more than he needs, because he is never happy with what he has got.

As Christians, we live with a different reality. If we have God as our Father, there is nothing to worry about. He will care for our needs now. We may not have everything that our contemporaries have, but we have something much more precious: the guarantee of our soul's eternal satisfaction in the presence of our God. And he promises to look after our every need in this life too. So no worries.

Do we really think we need more than this? We've seen how our culture has redefined our wants. Now we don't just need a roof over our heads; we need to own that roof. We don't just need clothing; it needs to be branded and new. We don't just need food; we need Tesco's Finest organic range.

There may be many good reasons why we own more than we need for survival, but we should be *content* with much less.

Indeed, we are able to be much more joyful than those who seek fulfilment from things that cannot make them truly happy.

So how might we apply this knowledge to John and Charlie?

Helping John

John still doesn't have a lot of money; his pay is still the same. His situation is tough, but he knows that the apostle Paul had it tougher and still managed to be thankful. Helping John to see that the new creation is where he will be truly happy will enable him to have realistic expectations of this life. At the same time, knowing that God has always provided for him and his family means that he doesn't need to worry about the future.

John's income doesn't go far, but it does cover the rent, put food on the table and provide clothes for his family. And being thankful and content certainly sounds better than being stressed and anxious all the time.

Helping Charlie

Most people would recognize that John has a difficult financial situation. But I hope we are beginning to see that Charlie has too. She never has any problem paying the bills, but her attitude to possessions shows that she isn't really content either. Charlie is spending a lot of money that God has given her so that she can build his kingdom, but instead she is busily building her own little empire.

We could help Charlie to see that her friends are chasing the trinkets and baubles of this world because they have no hope for the next. Once she knows what they are doing, she can decide to live differently. We can remind her of the surpassing worth of knowing Christ Jesus the Lord. We could help her to thank

God for giving her a job that allows her to live with money to spare, and suggest seeking wisdom from Christian friends about how she could use it to serve the kingdom of God.

I hope that you can see that the first part of dealing with any financial situation is to put it into God's perspective. That will help us to determine what is a problem with our circumstances and what is really a problem with our perception.

'God, not money, is Sovereign. Money – whether by its presence or absence – must never rule our lives,' says Randy Alcorn.[6]

What are you living for?

Who do you empathize with more, John or Charlie? Whatever our circumstances, we can all choose to live for now. Or we can invest our present in the future.

Do you really believe that God is providing all you need now and preparing a blissful eternity for you with him?

The Bible holds out a reward in heaven for those who invest in the heavenly enterprise. Both Paul (Philippians 4:17) and Jesus (Matthew 6:20) tell us that we can build a treasure trove of good things for ourselves in heaven, or we can choose to build one here. They do not allow us to do both.

Do we live as though we really believe this? Jesus says that we are to live to get to the new creation ourselves (Mark 8:34–38), by listening to his words and honouring them. That will mean taking him at his word in the Sermon on the Mount, and living to see the kingdom of God grow as the rule of Jesus is extended in the church. It means waiting for, longing for, Jesus to return.

It will mean being godly with our money *now*.

Study questions:

1. What do your spending habits tell you about what you think is really important?
2. What excites you most about the new creation? What do you find hardest to understand about it?
3. What would need to change in order for you to live wholeheartedly for the kingdom of God? Who could you ask to help you to do that?

CHAPTER 3

WHAT IS YOUR LIFE WORTH?

Ben works in finance. He leaves home by 7am and returns long after his three daughters are in bed. Lately he has been thinking that he works so much that he is not fulfilling his duty to raise his children to know and fear the Lord.

He has thought about going down to four days per week but fears that his job would remain just as busy, meaning longer days when he actually is at work. Ben has the opportunity to take time off unpaid. There is obviously a cost to this, both financially and with regard to his career, though neither means that he will be unable to feed and clothe the family. Should he exchange money that he could earn for time that he would like to spend with his family, or is that just irresponsible?

What is money, what do we do with it, and why? And who has the right to decide what we do with our time, money and energy? What does our current lifestyle tell us about what we think is important? And what do we need to change about our priorities to live in line with what Jesus thinks is important?

Let us start a little further back.

Information in numbers

Numbers capture information. I could give you a string of numbers, such as 123456, but they are mostly meaningless. But supposing I told you that these numbers were a telephone number, or the number string in the middle of a National Insurance number, or the sort code for a bank account?

Once we know the context from which these six digits come, we can employ the information that they represent. We might use the number to call a friend, or to fill in a form at the job centre, or to send money to someone else's bank account. We use numbers as a form of communication all the time. We are so accustomed to numbers carrying information that we often forget that they do so.

Let's suppose that I gave you the number 200. Without explaining the context, this number tells us nothing. However, if I told you that I spent £200 last month on food, it tells you something about how I live. If I told you that I spent £200 at Starbucks last month, the same number would tell you something very different. Numbers are like words: they are a language, and once we understand them in their context they can be very descriptive.

This is important, because the information that numbers capture helps us to get an unbiased view of how we live, what we think is important, and so forth. Imagine that you could step out of your life for a moment. Now imagine that we could describe your whole life in numbers – what you did with your time, your money and so on. What would you *want* those numbers to say about you?

What those numbers speak about is our discipleship or lack of it. 'Even a cursory reading of the New Testament shows [money and possessions] to be right at the heart of discipleship,' says Randy Alcorn.[1] In other words, when our lives are laid out before the bar of God's court, one of the things that will be scrutinized will be how we behaved with regard to money. It makes sense, then, for us to get to grips with what we are doing with money right now, while we have a chance to change our ways.

What is money?

The above might seem like a slightly elementary question. When I was about four years old, I went to our corner shop on my tricycle. I cycled into the shop, grabbed a chocolate bar and cycled out again. That was what I thought we did every time we went to the shops. I hadn't understood that a transaction was needed in order for possession of the chocolate to pass to me. Fortunately, the owner of the corner shop was more forgiving than my mother!

We all know what money looks like and what we can use it for. But what actually *is* it?

And the answer is . . .

Money is, in fact, you. Let me explain. We get money, usually, in exchange for the use of us. We work set hours for set pay. Money is really what we get back for using our time and skills for our employers. It is a measure of the *value* of our time. We each have only one lifetime, and the value we place on our life is reflected in how we use our time. In a sense, when we spend money we are really spending ourselves, the part of our lives that we spent acquiring that money.

If you think about that, it works in more contexts than money in exchange for time. Consider the student: university has many benefits. One of them is that people with degrees tend to earn more money than people without. In other words, one reason for spending three years earning nothing is that you can spend the rest of your working life earning more. The extra skills you have as a result of your education make you more employable, and that means you can charge more for the hours you sell to an employer: your rate of pay.

In a way we might say that:

$$Money = Time \times (Skills + Energy)$$

That is, the money I earn this week is a product of my time and my rate of pay. So the prospective student might well ask, 'Is the income I forego for three years, and the debt I accrue, worth the additional income I will earn from my shorter career?' (We will think more about this in chapter 7.)

So what?

I wanted to draw our attention to this because there is a danger that, in a book about money, we can easily make an unrealistic distinction. Decisions about money are never made in isolation from other considerations, and we mustn't pretend that they are.

Consider the following illustration. I could write in this book that all Christians should give as much as they can financially to their church. That would imply that no Christian would ever make a decision that reduced their giving. But in that case, why would any Christian ever have kids? A lot of money, time and skills that could be used in the service of the gospel are now eaten up in raising children. Why, too, would anyone leave a well-paid secular job in order to train for the more poorly paid ministry?

Here is the danger. In reality, we never make decisions based purely on economic considerations. And that is why I have tried to set this discussion in the wider context of living the Christian life. We need to avoid establishing rules that are both unbiblical and unhelpful for making godly decisions.

As we look at this subject, we need to remember that money is no more important than time or skills used in the service of God. All are important, so we need to think a bit about them all.

When you spend money, time and energy, you spend yourself. You spend a limited resource that is valuable to you. So what you spend your money, time and energy *on* tells you a lot about what you think is important.

When £10 is not £10

People will make different decisions when faced with the same choice, because their context is different. Consider the following extreme example, which I hope is unrealistic, but makes the point clearly.

Imagine two people who both work five days a week. They work the same hours, but one is paid £5,000 per year and the other £50,000. Suppose I were to offer each of them another £5,000 per year, but they had to work Saturdays as well to get it. What do you think each of them would say?

> *When you spend money, time and energy, you spend yourself. You spend a limited resource that is valuable to you.*

It's the same amount of money for the same time to both of them. So why would one say 'yes' and the other 'no'? The answer is in the value of the money, relative to the value of the time.

For a person earning £5,000, the time is almost immaterial; it doesn't matter when compared to the fact that they can't pay the rent and put enough food on the table. The additional money is worth their life because it enables them to sustain that life.

On the other hand, the person who earns £50,000 can already put food on the table and pay the rent. They don't *need* to work on Saturdays. As a result, they will consider the value of their time at the weekend and might understandably conclude that time with friends or family is worth more than £5,000.

The real value of money to any individual is determined by what it costs to get the money and what it enables them to buy.

You can see how this connects to what we saw in the last chapter. The things that are needful for us are very important. So we exchange a lot of time to get the money to buy those things because without them we will die.

The changing value of time and money

In the above example, £5,000 was very valuable to the person with the poorly paid job because it bought them the ability to sustain life. The day per week lost in exchange was almost irrelevant.

The principle here is that the *value* of time and money depends on how much of it you have got. At the beginning of the week we all have 168 hours and no money. Let us say that I need £300 per week to cover my essentials, and 70 hours per week to sleep and eat (also essentials). What I have are a lot of hours in which to eat and sleep, and what I need is money to pay for my food and shelter.

What I really need is a job that allows me to earn enough to cover my essentials without demanding more hours than I am prepared to give. Let us say, for the sake of argument, that I can earn £10 per hour, ignoring tax. I will want to work at least 30 hours per week because that covers my essentials.

In this scenario, I would still have 68 hours in the week to fill with something and no money left after essentials. So again I put a value on my time and sell some of it to my employer. The fewer hours I have left, the more I will want from my employer for those hours. At the same time, I will need some money to be able to do things in the remaining hours.

So, let us say that I am willing to work the next 18 hours per week for £15 per hour. That would give me 50 hours left and £270 to spend in those hours.

And so it goes on. The less time I have, the more precious it is, and the more money I want in exchange for that time. Eventually, time becomes more precious than the money I can earn, and I stop selling my time to my employer.

The rate of pay and the level of essentials and so forth will change from person to person. Yet for all of us, there are three parts to our time: that which we want to sell to cover essentials (A), that which we *might* sell or *might* use ourselves (B), and that which we need to keep so that we can sleep and eat (C). The list of essentials in C will also include time with family, at church and so on.

Money value of time

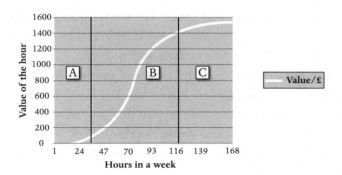

In section A we need to sell the time in order to live, and we sell it cheaply. At the other end of the graph, we would be unwilling to sell any of the time in section C without considerable compensation, because that is time we need for the essentials to stay alive. What would someone have to pay you in order to buy your eating and sleeping time from you?

How we behave with money and time in each section will be very different. In section A, for example, we need money rather than time. No question. The opposite is true in section C. But in section B it is either one or the other, depending upon which is more attractive. And that is based on which matters more to us.

Marginal time

The area that we most want to focus on is section B. We don't *need* to work or do anything else with the time there, but the fact is that we will end up doing *something*. The question we need to ask is: what ought to be my priorities for that time? Some of it is likely to be taken up by work because our employer wants us to work a minimum number of hours. But, still, how many hours should we be willing to work? And how ought we to use our time and money outside work?

'What is most important to you?' could be rephrased as 'How do you use your marginal time?' Do we spend all this time at work, indicating that our job is most important? Or do we spend it on a relationship or following a sports team?

We might call this 'marginal time and money'. We could ask, 'How do you spend the last £10 or the last hour that you have to spare?' What is so precious to you that you would choose to do that one thing over and above anything else?

What is so valuable that we would spend our life on it? That is the question that we want to keep asking all through this book. And to answer it, we will also need to think about *who* decides what is important.

Who decides what matters?

At the start of this book we saw that our culture has a set of priorities that express themselves in very now-focused attitudes. And in chapter 2 we saw that God is future-focused, looking forward to that day when he will bless his people in his place for ever. We now see that what really matters to us can be gauged by how we use our marginal time and money.

So what principle ought to govern our use of time, money and energy if we are going to live for the new creation? That brings us to our next Bible principle.

> **Bible principle 2:**
> God owns everything

God's rule and the gospel

One of the most foundational Christian truths is that God made everything: 'In the beginning, God created the heavens and the earth' (Genesis 1:1). God stood outside the universe and created it by the strength of his own will, from his own imagination and by the power of his spoken word.

Since God made the universe, it follows that it belongs to him. In Genesis 1, God expresses his authority over creatures by naming them. And in Genesis, the universe responds appropriately by doing exactly what God tells it to do. Except that, in Genesis 3, humankind decides not to. The consequences of Adam and Eve's disobedience are catastrophic, to say the least. And from that point on in history, it is clear that humanity is fighting against God for the right to rule.

God is clear from the beginning to the end of the Bible that the great problem that prevents us from being blessed in his presence is our rebellion. That is why God's great rescue plan is focused on the penalty-taking death of Jesus on our behalf (Isaiah 53:4–6).

Rebellion is sin, and God has punished sin in Jesus so that we humans can be blessed. Jesus' death redeems us *from* sin. But it also redeems us *for* obedience to the gospel. So the apostle Peter says that we are saved 'according to the foreknowledge of God the Father, in the sanctification of the Spirit, *for obedience to Jesus Christ* and for sprinkling with his blood' (1 Peter 1:2, emphasis mine).

We Christians are therefore not free to make up our own ways of thinking and living. Jesus died to bring us back under the rule of our God. That is why we speak of Jesus as Lord. He owns everything and everyone, and everyone ought to submit to his rule.

One of the questions I am most often asked is: 'What should I do with my money?' It is not a great question because it is so full of conflict. On the one hand, it asserts that there is a moral element to my use of money, a 'should', a right and a wrong thing to do. That is to say, we are asking what God expects us to do.

On the other hand, we are asserting our ownership of our possessions. What does God think I ought to do with the things that are 'mine'? We end up asserting two wills, God's and our own, whenever we think about money decisions. A much better question to ask is: 'What does God think I should do with the money and possessions he has entrusted to me as his steward?' OK, so it isn't as succinct, but I think it's a lot more biblical.

God owns everything by right, including us, the money he has given us, and our relationships. And he has bought us, redeemed us from slavery to sin and death, at the cost of his own precious Son. So he owns us twice over. This means that, even in a world that ignores God, we are to make his priorities ours.

God owns us

This could be a terrifying truth if it weren't for the lavishness of God's love for his people. We see it throughout the Bible, and specifically in the Old Testament, as God patiently woos back his bride, Israel. We see it especially in the cross, which we deserved and which Jesus bore in our place, even while we were God's enemies (Romans 5:11; cf. 1 John 4:10). Indeed, discipleship starts when we renounce our right to control those things that belong to God (Luke 14:33).

God has the right to command how we use all 168 hours of every week. He has the right of a sovereign over his money, of which we are stewards, not owners. 'When we have this perspective, spending and saving decisions are equally as spiritual as giving decisions.'[2] The Bible is replete with commands to watch our hearts. We might want to resist the rule of King Jesus in certain areas, and money is likely to be one of them. So we need to remember what is at stake if we refuse to let God be our king: our place in the new creation.

Consider 1 Corinthians 6:9–11:

> **Or do you not know that the unrighteous will not inherit the kingdom of God? Do not be deceived: neither the sexually immoral, nor idolaters, nor adulterers, nor men who practise homosexuality, nor thieves, nor the greedy, nor drunkards, nor revilers, nor swindlers will inherit the kingdom of God. And such were some of you. But you were washed, you were sanctified, you were justified in the name of the Lord Jesus Christ and by the Spirit of our God.**

All manner of ungodly people join the church. But in becoming Christians, we are washed from all unrighteousness, for a godly life.

Craig Blomberg comments:

> **In 1 Corinthians 6:10 Paul proclaims that such [greedy/ covetous] people, if in fact this is their characteristic**

lifestyle rather than merely an occasional lapse, simply will not inherit the kingdom of God![3]

So how we use our marginal time is of eternal significance because it tells us whether or not we are really living for the future we will share with God. The things that dominate our time and money reflect the things that dominate our hearts and show us where we will spend eternity.

God's purpose for the end of time

When Jesus returns to judge the world, he will bring with him the new creation in which all his people will enjoy him for ever. As we wait for that day, we are to live with him as our king, making all our decisions based on his priorities for our lives.

In the next chapter, we will think about God's priorities for money in particular. But before we get there, let's focus on God's priorities for this world *until* Jesus comes back.

God's priorities for now

Given that God wants people to be in the new creation with him, we might ask what he would have us do now. Let's consider this under two broad headings that Jesus himself gave us (Matthew 22:37, 39; Mark 12:30–31).

Love the Lord your God

Jesus tells us that the greatest commandment is to love God with all our heart, mind, soul and strength. We are to be fully engaged, with every faculty we have, all the time, in loving God.

In the context of the Gospels, this means especially loving the one he sent to die on our behalf, Jesus Christ. It will mean loving the things he said and did, and doing all that he commanded (John 5:23).

It will mean honouring Jesus as Saviour and Lord, first by putting our trust in him and then by turning from our rebellion (see 1 Thessalonians 1:9–10).

And it will mean ensuring that we *keep* trusting Jesus, obeying him day by day (Hebrews 3:12–15).

Not only does Matthew 22 demand our wholehearted devotion, it also requires that the honour of the Lord Jesus should be our most pressing concern. This is particularly important when we consider the second part of the saying.

Love your neighbour as yourself
Imagine the scenario. An old friend has fallen on hard times – homeless, penniless, jobless and godless. Make a list of all the things that you would want to do to love that friend. Clearly you would want to meet each of his physical needs. Yet at the top of that list will be the desire to help him become reconciled to the Father in heaven. There are three reasons for this:

First, if we love the Lord our God as our first priority, then we will want, more than anything, for him to be honoured as he should be. It is scandalous for our friend to continue to live in rebellion against God, and we cannot claim to be fulfilling the greatest commandment if we are not concerned about this.

Secondly, we follow the model Jesus gave us of loving God and his neighbour. Jesus certainly met the needs of those around him, but *never* to the exclusion of preaching the arrival of the kingdom and the need to repent (Mark 1:14–15, 38). Indeed, every good deed of Jesus in the Gospels acts as an illustration of the things he was teaching.

Thirdly, we cannot claim to love people by meeting only those needs that *they* recognize, while *we* know that Jesus is coming back to judge them. It is folly to pretend that their biggest need is marriage counselling or debt advice when they really need Jesus. Not only will he solve their biggest problem now but, in the new creation, he will solve *all* their problems, permanently. All our other work is like putting a sticking plaster on a severed limb if we just make their life comfortable as they stumble blindly towards hell.

In other words, God's priorities focus on a world in rebellion against him, and his desire to see people reconciled to himself through Jesus' death. Ours ought to be the same. God knows that the restoration of a relationship with him is the only way to lasting blessing.

Of course, our compassion for the plight of those made in the image of God will overflow in acts of kindness. We need to remember that the biblical definition of love (1 John 4:10) is the giving of oneself: Jesus dying on the cross to restore sinners to God.

Diagnosing priorities

I'd like to think that my priorities reflect those we have just discussed. I have found it helpful, however, to ask a few questions of myself to test whether or not this is the case. You might find these useful too.

How would I feel about losing X? For example, my job. If I were offered the same salary and hours to do something un-pleasant, would I be willing to do it? Clearly we all choose our career for a reason, but does the job we do mean too much to us?

The same question could be asked of something less essential than work. If I had to stop playing football (and age is catching up with me), would I be willing to give it up? I suspect that there are many treasured things that we are less willing to give up than we ought to be, things that have perhaps joined God on the throne of our lives, even if they haven't completely displaced him.

If I had to choose between X and Y, which would I give up? A similar question to the last one: which of our treasured hobbies and possessions is most treasured? What would you be prepared to sacrifice in order to go to the game, go shopping, or watch your favourite show?

How do I actually spend 168 hours per week/my salary? The answer may seem obvious, but I suspect that many of us spend a lot of time and money on things that we don't actually notice. How much time do you honestly spend watching TV? Or on the Wii? It would be easy to spend hours every day on those things, precious hours that belong to Jesus. I am not suggesting that relaxing is a bad thing, and we all need to find ways of doing that, but how much time should we spend on those things?

What matters most?

Some of the things that are precious to us ought to be so. My wife and sons are really precious to me, and so they should be. A good question to ask, therefore, is whether the things that matter to us really ought to matter. Another good question is: 'In 100 million years, will it matter that I . . . ?'

If the answer is no, then we need to be willing to replace that thing with something that really does matter. This doesn't mean that every minute of every day we need to be doing something obviously kingdom-related, but it does mean a willingness to shape our lives and choices around what matters to God.

So what is most valuable to you? And will it seem that precious when Jesus returns?

Study questions:

1. What do you find hardest about God's right to rule? How does Jesus' willingness to die for you help with this?
2. How might thinking of money as part of the life God has given to you help you to be wiser with it?
3. What are some of the things that are important to you that you would be willing to give up for the sake of King Jesus?

CHAPTER 4

GOD'S PRIORITIES FOR YOUR MONEY

Geoff is caught in a quandary. He earns a reasonable living, and after essentials has about £5,000 per year left over. He is a keen follower of Jesus and knows that he ought to give much of this to Christian causes.

However, Geoff's parents have recently retired and are struggling to meet their basic needs on a small state pension. For health reasons, neither of his parents can go out to work. Geoff knows that they ought to have prepared better for their retirement, and he doesn't feel it is right to take money out of the church's share to support them. On the other hand, they *are* his parents and he feels he has a responsibility to care for them, as they cared for him when he was growing up. What should he do?

We all have limited financial resources, so how should we best order our priorities to reflect God's concerns? What might a life shaped by God's priorities look like? We'll also think about some practical considerations. And as God has called us to be trust-worthy stewards of his money (1 Corinthians 4:2), we will need to think about what trustworthiness will look like.

Responsibilities and concerns

Our primary concern until we get to the new creation ought to be loving the Lord with all our being and loving our neighbours as ourselves. This is complicated by the great many physical needs that are felt, personally, locally and globally. In a hypothetical world in which I controlled all the world's resources, I would make sure that everyone got to hear the gospel and had a full stomach every day (though, interestingly, God does control all resources and *doesn't* do this). When resources are unlimited, we obviously don't need to order our priorities.

But none of us has unlimited resources, and there are seemingly unlimited needs. One-third of the world's population lives below a reasonable poverty line. Even by 1982, 200 million of the world's poorest people professed some sort of Christian faith,[1] and with the recent growth of the church in the two-thirds world that number is likely to have grown substantially.

At the same time, hundreds of millions of people do not even have the Bible in their own language, let alone indigenous churches to attend. The need to fund missions has never been greater.

Given our limited resources, what should the order of our priorities be? Broadly, we can think of our responsibilities as illustrated in the diagram on the next page.

The circles in the middle take priority over those further out. Within each circle, spiritual care (relationship to God) takes precedence over physical needs (relationship to creation). Let us think back to chapter 3: our first commandment is to love God, for his honour and our right relationship with him. The second commandment is to love our neighbours, which will certainly include wanting them to be restored to a relationship with God for his honour, because that is what Jesus did and because it is in their best interests.

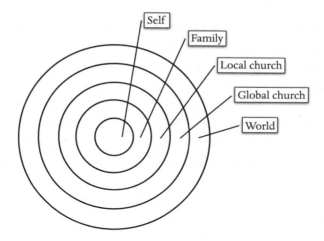

Though the diagram might seem counter-intuitive, let us think about how that will work out in practice.

Looking after number one

Once we realize that our first concern is how everyone relates to God, it makes sense that the first thing to sort out is our own relationship with God.

We have already seen in Philippians how the apostle Paul counted everything else as loss if only he could remain a Christian (Philippians 3:8). We have heard Jesus say that a man would give up everything he has on the day of judgment when he realizes that, by rejecting Jesus, he has missed out on eternal life (Mark 8:36–37). And we have heard Jesus tell us that the most important commandment is to love God with our whole being (Matthew 22:37; cf. Mark 12:30).

For me to take care of my physical needs at the expense of my relationship with God is foolish, to say the least. In the end I will have to face death anyway. It is much more important to prioritize the basis on which I face that death.

Investing in our relationship with God is of paramount importance. You might, nevertheless, suggest that this is awfully selfish. Would it not be more godly to put my wife's relationship with God ahead of my own? Yet it is only when *my* relationship with God is strong that I am able to serve others in a sacrificial way.

So take my relationship with my wife, for example. I am most likely to serve her sacrificially, to forgive her wrongs, to ask forgiveness for mine, and to do so without selfish motives, when I am deeply aware of the grace of God to me in Jesus. As I reflect on his love for me, I am better able to show that love to my family and my church and the world in the same way (though not to the same degree). The light of God is strongest in us when we draw nearest to the source of that light: Jesus.

It might be worth reflecting on how much, or how little, time we spend with the Lord in our devotions each day, how much time we spend hearing from God in sermons and through Christian books. If we invest little time in our relationship with God, is that because it doesn't really matter to us? Does the way I use my time and money suggest for example that I am more interested in feeding my body than in nourishing my soul?

Family next

Spiritual needs first

Again, it may seem counter-intuitive to put the family next. When you think about it, however, it makes perfect sense. The family is the place where biblical instruction is meant to take place (Exodus 12:24–27; Ephesians 6:4). The home is to be a small church, with the father as the senior pastor (though, of course, many homes do not fit this pattern exactly, and that is God's plan for their good). Taking care of the family's spiritual welfare of course includes getting involved in a church that will teach all the members of the family. But attending church is only a small part of teaching and modelling godly living.

But let us suppose that we do not live near a church where we and our family will be fed spiritually. I believe that church is more important than what school our children go to, where we work and what sort of house we live in. In fact, all physical welfare issues (though by no means irrelevant) ought to be secondary to the need to be constantly encouraged to grow in our relationship with God. So we should make a considerable financial sacrifice in order to move to an area where such a church exists. When push comes to shove, what are our real priorities for our family?

Physical needs
It is really tricky to put any list of biblical priorities in order where physical needs are concerned, and you might have thought I would have listed church next. But as I look at the Bible, it seems to me that the family is very important. Let me show you why.

In 1 Timothy 3, Paul gives a long list of criteria that a man must meet in order to be considered fit to lead in the church. Among them is the following:

He must manage his own household well, with all dignity keeping his children submissive, for if someone does not know how to manage his own household, how will he care for God's church? (1 Timothy 3:4–5)

The household in the first century could mean all the extended family who relied on the family business or estate for their sustenance. That could have been up to thirty people. Managing the household, then, is not just managing to keep the children submissive, but it really does mean managing, in a business sense – making sure that the household functions so that everyone is fed.

If you can't manage your own home, you are not fit to manage the family of God's people. There is a note in here for pastors that we shall return to later.

But all Paul is doing in 1 Timothy 3 is giving a list of criteria that he would expect any mature Christian to satisfy. We should expect our leaders to be godly. But we shouldn't expect them to have a different standard of godliness from everyone else.

That seems to be the point Paul goes on to make in 1 Timothy 5. He imagines a situation where a widow has fallen on hard times. She is unable to work and so unable to eat. Who has responsibility for her well-being?

> **Honour widows who are truly widows. But if a widow has children or grandchildren, let them first learn to show godliness to their own *household* and to make some return to their parents, for this is pleasing in the sight of God. She who is truly a widow, left all alone, has set her hope on God and continues in supplications and prayers night and day, but she who is self-indulgent is dead even while she lives. Command these things as well, so that they may be without reproach. But if anyone does not provide for his relatives, and especially for members of his household, he has denied the faith and is worse than an unbeliever.**
> (1 Timothy 5:3–8, emphasis mine)

The church is to look after the Christian who is all alone, according to verse 3 and verse 5. But if that person has relatives, then they are to take responsibility for them. It is a matter of godliness to look after elderly relatives, just as it is a matter of godliness for parents to look after their children. The household clearly includes parents (verse 4), so there is no escaping the force of verse 8.

In fact, Paul looks at the pagan society around him, a society that lacks the restraint of a Christian heritage, and is able to say, 'Even *they* know that you are responsible for your relatives.' Not to look after your family wouldn't just be sub-Christian, but sub-pagan too. I take it that the same thing applies to us today.[2]

Whether or not your family are believers, you have a responsibility to ensure that they are properly looked after.

Of course, the scenario might be reversed, so that the Christian becomes the one in need. What happens when the rest of the family are unbelievers and do not recognize their responsibility? I take it that the church would want to look after its own, just as the early church did (Acts 4:32–35). Indeed, there will be those who are disowned by their family for their faith in Jesus, and we must look after them as though there was no family to look after them.

Caution!

However, two words of caution: first, we are responsible for supplying what is needed, not necessarily everything that our families might want. 'A need is a necessity of life – food, clothing and shelter. A want is anything more than a need,' says Mark Lloydbottom.[3] God has promised to meet the needs of all who trust in him. Often the way he will do this is through the generosity of others who trust in him.

Secondly, we are not to look after those who could look after themselves but won't. The Bible is full of cautions that if a man will not work he shouldn't eat (e.g. 2 Thessalonians 3:10; Ecclesiastes 4:5).

The Christian is responsible for his family. Consider Geoff in our opening example. Would the church miss his giving if he gave to his parents? Well, probably a little, but the rest of the congregation ought to meet the needs of the church, because all their money belongs to God.

On the other hand, if Geoff gives the money to the church, then there is nobody else to support his parents and they might well starve. For that reason we ought to meet the needs of our relatives ahead of our giving, providing they are in genuine need.

I should say that Geoff's care for the physical needs of his family will be constant and may well come ahead of any opportunity he has to care for them spiritually. Our priorities say nothing about the order in which we meet needs, but everything about our key *aims* in caring for others. It is all about keeping the central things central.

Many of us will have dependent relatives at some point in our lives, and we will need to consider planning for the long term ourselves. Nevertheless, for many of us, our responsibility to family will still leave us with resources to spare.

The local church

If it is our priority to find a church that supports our relationship with God, it makes perfect sense that we should want to support that church as a response. We should want to do everything that we can to encourage our ministers to keep preaching Christ (Colossians 1:28), including giving them our time and money. 'If we are giving to a church . . . this is only charity. But if we are giving to the Lord, our Creator, Provider and Saviour in love and gratitude, it is an act of worship,' says Keith Tondeur.[4]

Two ways to care

There are two things that we ought to be engaged in if the church is to stay faithful to Jesus. The first is to speak the truth to one another. According to Ephesians 4, the thing that really builds the church into one mature body of Christ is that *everyone* speaks the truth to one another (Ephesians 4:12–16). Our responsibility to the local church includes caring for the rest of the congregation and allowing them to look after us as we seek to help one another to know and follow Jesus better.

Secondly, given the importance of the local church as the place where we are nurtured in our faith and serve, it is also critical that we make sure that we are taught correctly. Indeed, in Ephesians 4, the work of the congregation is impossible without the ministers leading the church properly (Ephesians 4:11–12). Since God is concerned about our eternal salvation, it makes sense that we should be as well.

That is why the Bible is at pains to say that Christian workers are entitled to be supported by the church they serve:

One who is taught the word must share all good things with the one who teaches. (Galatians 6:6)

If we want a healthy church, then we also need a healthy pulpit, because it is only as we keep hearing and believing the words of Jesus that we remain in him, the source of life (John 15:1–8).

It makes sense then to strengthen the ministry in our local church with our time, energy and money. The farmer who neglects to care for his crops is a fool, since they feed him and his family. So it is with us and the church. We ought to be giving to provide the means with which to pay church staff and other costs, so that nothing distracts them from the crucial work of preaching the gospel.

Someone suggested to me that a more biblical model would be for the minister to support himself, as Paul did. However, a closer look suggests that Paul did this in missionary contexts (1 Thessalonians 2:7; 2 Corinthians 11:9). Indeed, in 2 Corinthians 11:9, Paul says that the reason he was able not to burden the Corinthians was that the Macedonian church supported his ministry. Paul expected help from the established churches, as in Philippians 4 and Romans 15.

It seems fairer to suggest, then, that in a pioneering situation, in which a church is very young, it would be appropriate for the minister to support himself, or seek assistance from more mature churches. But this is not so in an established church, which will be the context for most of us.

All things in common

In John 13:35 Jesus tells us that when we love one another as a church, we are being so radical that the watching world will conclude that we belong to him. Genuine, sacrificial, generous love is so rare in our culture that only Jesus' followers are able to show it.

It seems, for example, that the brand new church formed on the day of Pentecost was so transformed by the gospel, so aware of its unity, that:

> **they devoted themselves to the apostles' teaching and the fellowship, to the breaking of bread and the prayers. And awe came upon every soul, and many wonders and signs were being done through the apostles. And all who believed were together and had all things in common. And they were selling their possessions and belongings and distributing the proceeds to all, as any had need.** (Acts 2:42–45; cf. 4:32–35)

Nobody got possessive about his own land, his own stuff. It all belonged to God and could be sold at the drop of a hat to care for any brothers in need. We have already seen that there were strict limits on who qualified for aid in 1 Timothy 5, but if you qualified then it was always forthcoming.[5] That doesn't mean that there was ever total equality: some owned land that could be sold later, while others had very little.[6] Still, they were committed to seeing that the gap between rich and poor in the church was greatly reduced.

> *Tragically, the sort of life that we see in the early church in Acts often seems as far from us as it was from the culture of their day.*

Tragically, the sort of life that we see in the early church in Acts often seems as far from us as it was from the culture of their day.

So far, so . . .

So far we have seen that our priorities ought to be to fund what is needed, spiritually and physically, by ourselves, our families and our congregations. Sometimes this is as far as our eyesight reaches. But sometimes we see beyond the local church to a world in need. There is, however, a much-neglected point in between which should challenge both those who see no needs beyond the doors of their church and those who are fully engaged in a world in great need.

The global church

The local church is only ever an expression of the whole body of Christ throughout the world. Those of us who have travelled to another country and been welcomed into a church fellowship as a brother or sister in Christ will know the truth of this. It is one of the reasons why the church has always supported mission to other parts of the world, just as Paul asked the Romans to do as he went on to Spain (Romans 15:24).

Our concern for the spiritual care of the global church might mean any number of things. Or it might mean supporting theological students and colleges in areas where indigenous leaders are needed for the church. Or it might mean sending missionaries overseas. Or it might mean ourselves going to other parts of the world with our useful skills.

If we are really to care for the spiritual needs of a world that is lost, then we need a global church that is preaching the gospel message and living it out in local fellowships.

Your abundance at the present time
Alongside the desire that the global church should be equipped for faithful living, we ought to be concerned about the great disparity in physical means between churches. In Acts 11, Luke records for us the arrival of the prophet Agabus at Antioch to warn of a global famine. This would affect the whole world, Christians and non-Christians, Jews and Gentiles alike. The response of the church?

> **So the disciples determined, everyone according to his ability, to send relief to the brothers living in Judea. And they did so, sending it to the elders by the hand of Barnabas and Saul.** (Acts 11:29–30)

Indeed, Saul (Paul) spent some years travelling around the Mediterranean, seeking support for the Jerusalem church from all the churches he had established. They presumably chose the Judean church because they were already heavily persecuted and therefore least likely to be able to support themselves in the famine. This is illustrated by Paul in 2 Corinthians when he encourages that church to dig deeply for the famine relief effort:

> **For I do not mean that others should be eased and you burdened, but that as a matter of fairness your abundance at the present time should supply their need, so that their abundance may supply your need,**

**that there may be fairness. As it is written,
'Whoever gathered much had nothing left over,
and whoever gathered little had no lack.'**
(2 Corinthians 8:13–15)

There is a great challenge here for us as a church in the West: will we share our material blessings with God's people elsewhere? Is the church of God, wherever it is found, precious enough to us that we would give up some of our physical comforts now? Famines and persecution remain real experiences for God's people around the world. Paul would have us read 2 Corinthians 8 – 9 as though it were written to us as well.

Responding to a world in need

The response of the church in Acts 11 to the famine was to care for their fellow believers, reflecting the response of the church throughout the Bible: radical care for those in her midst. This is not to play down the massive challenges of a suffering world, or to suggest that we do nothing to help.

Rather, it is to suggest that we need to be radical in caring for the church first, remembering that the love of Christ shown within the church is a testimony, drawing people in. The world notices how counter-cultural we are with 'our' money as we care for all those in our fellowships.

And this is not to suggest that we should not care passionately for others around us. As we saw earlier, if a friend came to you in need you would certainly help – but always remembering their greatest need is Jesus.

For every passage where we are told to 'do good to all', there is an equally emphatic 'especially to the household of faith' (Galatians 6:10). The word 'especially' must mean that we either care for the church ahead of the world, or care for the church in extra ways that we don't care for the world. The church comes first. I fear that this is a blind spot for the Western church, to the great detriment of our witness to the world. We must not let our concerns be driven by what is apparent to our eyes, nor by what is acceptable to our culture, but by what the Scriptures tell us. We are to walk by faith, not sight.

Whatever else we do for our neighbours, we must keep their need for Jesus front and centre. That there is crime, broken relationships and social disorder in a society that ignores God is not a surprise. That there will be none of these problems in the new creation shows us that the gospel has a response to every concern we might have – and that the answer is to put our trust in Jesus for a perfect future.

A response to grace

And all this is a response to the amazing grace of God poured out on us, his undeserving people. As we grasp the extent of Christ's love for us, as we grasp the eternal glory that is prepared for us, so we can pour ourselves into serving the mission of our God to his world.

That makes a lot of sense, doesn't it? The more we understand how much Jesus did for us, in suspending his heavenly glory to become a servant, and to die a criminal's death for us, the more willing we will be to pour ourselves out for others. The more we appreciate the ongoing generosity of God to us, the more willing we will be to give freely from all that we already have (2 Corinthians 9). That brings us to our third biblical principle:

> **Bible principle 3:**
> Be like your heavenly Father: generous

That is exactly what Paul argues for in 2 Corinthians 9. In verse 8 Paul says: 'God is able to make all grace abound to you, so that having all sufficiency in all things at all times, you may abound in every good work.'

Four times Paul uses the word 'all' to highlight that our God is so generous that there is never a time or place when his generosity is not poured out to us. God can make his grace 'abound' to us, to overflow. Having this great sufficiency, we too can abound in our good works poured out to others. We are to be generous as our Father in heaven is generous.

This is not for a second to suggest that God's generosity is necessarily financial, that if you give, then God will give you more of the same thing (never the promise in the New Testament). But he is no man's debtor. The promise of verse 11 is that we 'will be enriched in every way to be generous in every way', and it is a shame that we are so slow to be rich towards others, knowing that our Father has deeper pockets than we do.

Our priority, then, is the salvation of souls. And yet we will not want to neglect the body. That is why being like our Father will mean wanting to meet physical needs as well as spiritual ones – our Father, after all, always looks after those things for us. Alcorn puts it like this: 'Giving is becoming like our Father: it isn't just his way of raising money – it is his way of raising children.'[7]

Let's now focus on a current, real-life scenario and see how we can apply some godly wisdom.

Study questions:

1. What surprises you about God's priorities? How do they differ from what you have historically thought they were?
2. What responsibilities have you become aware of during this chapter? How can you begin to plan to meet them?
3. Which favourite verses of Scripture could you memorize to remind yourself of how generous God has been to you already?

CHAPTER 5

GETTING OUT OF DEBTORS' PRISON

Sophie works in technologies in Bristol. She has a soft spot for all things new and shiny and is rarely self-controlled when it comes to gadgets. Sophie has a couple of store cards with substantial balances, as well as a credit card. She never struggles to meet the minimum payments and she never quite runs out of money.

Lately, however, she has become convinced that her spending habits indicate that her priorities are in the wrong place. She knows that all she earns is God's money and she wants to honour him with it.

At the same time, Sophie is thinking about buying a house and she will need a substantial mortgage. What should she do to get out of debt, and the bad habits that landed her there in the first place? And is it OK to get that mortgage?

Many of us remain for a long time ignorant of the damaging patterns of behaviour we are engaged in. It is often only when a major transition happens in our lives that we become aware of them. Consider Sophie's scenario.

Not an isolated incident

Most developed countries are currently struggling with massive national and personal debts – we've seen that this is certainly true of the UK. Sophie's situation is typical for a generation of reasonably wealthy young people with few commitments. Reasonably well-off she may be, but honouring God with *his* money she is not.

Unsecured loans

An unsecured loan is a liability to pay later an amount lent to you, against which you have not pledged an asset of at least equal value. For example, imagine that you book flights for your summer holiday on your credit card. You travel, and upon your return you still owe money for the flights. The item you bought cannot be returned and refunded (unless you can travel through time), but you will still need to pay off the debt. You have offered no security against the possibility of default, and in exchange the loan is made at a high rate of interest.

Sophie has at least three unsecured loans, evidence that she has been living beyond her means. Furthermore, making the minimum payments each month means that the lender gets to charge obscene interest rates on the balance. Her lack of control has led to her paying a lot more for her goods than she realized they would cost.

This sort of debt is acquired to buy things that we cannot afford. When we buy food, for example, we think that we are buying something that *must* be bought in order to survive. However, living on credit means that there is an underlying problem: we haven't actually got the means month by month to buy what we need. In that case, the solution is not credit but seeking help from others about how to reduce our outgoings or increase our income.

If you find yourself in this sort of situation, why not seek professional help from an agency such as Credit Action (www.creditaction.org.uk)? Its staff often counsel people who *think* that they have financial problems, when really they just need to change a few basic habits.

First steps
Sophie needs a plan to get clear of debt. But before she can make one, she needs to know what her debts are and what they cost her. She needs to make a list. By listing their size and interest rate, she can see the most expensive ones and so identify which one is her highest priority. She may find it helpful to include all her substantial assets, including savings and any saleable possessions. Remember that it all belongs to God.

Consider the table below, with debt amounts in brackets:

Item	Value now/£	Interest rate	Value in 1 yr/£	Adjusted value in 1 yr/£
House deposit	15,000	3%	15,450	15,450
Savings	2,000	3%	2,060	–
Store cards	(1,000)	24%	(1,240)	–
Credit cards	(1,500)	18%	(1,770)	(590)
Student loans	(15,000)	1%	(15,150)	(15,150)
Total	(500)		(650)	(290)

As the final two columns show, by using her savings, which are generating only 3% interest in any case, to repay credit and store cards that are charging much more, Sophie can reduce her balance by £360 over the next year. Additionally, she might consider getting a loan from the bank to cover any debts at higher rates of interest. She should remember, however, that such loans often do not allow you to pay back the debt more quickly without charging penalties. It therefore becomes harder to get debt-free quickly. It also means that, although the rate of interest is lower, the amount of interest paid may be about the same over time because the debt cannot be repaid in a short period.

Sophie would be wise to think about any items she owns that she might sell to further reduce her debts. That would include considering using the house deposit she has saved in order to repay her outstanding loans.

Finally, she needs to develop a strategy for paying off the debts. It makes sense to pay off the most expensive ones first (those at the highest rates of interest), and she should consider how to reduce her normal expenditure to free up money each month in order to make additional repayments to reduce the debt as quickly as possible.

Changing behaviour

What Sophie most needs is a change in lifestyle. By following the advice in this book, Sophie will be able to identify which are her real needs and prioritize those when she gets her pay cheque every month.

Assuming that she can cover her necessities, she then needs to factor in repaying current debts in order to clear them. If she has consolidated all her debts into a bank loan, that loan will be repayable at a fixed rate and over a fixed period.

After that she can think about saving and her responsibilities to her family, and giving. Only then should she think about spending on discretionary items.

If you find yourself in Sophie's situation, it is definitely worth taking advice from a professional advisor or someone else whose financial integrity you respect. This person will help you to form, and stick to, a plan. Without accountability, change is always much harder.

Mortgage

Sophie is also thinking about getting a mortgage. Isn't that just like any other debt? Wouldn't that be really unwise? We'll ignore her loans and consider the issue of mortgages in isolation.

A mortgage is a type of debt, but secured against the land you are buying. If you default on making payments, then the property is taken away in lieu of payment. Almost nobody buys property outright, and so everyone tends to acquire a mortgage. But *should* we?

There are a number of reasons for buying property. I want to suggest that buying a house because you want to, or because everyone else does, is not a satisfactory reason. It is not required in the Bible that people own their own homes. We need, therefore, to move away from ownership for ownership's sake.

However, as an investment, property can make a lot of sense. Businesses borrow money to invest in new machines to make new products in order to make money. In a similar way, property ownership could be an investment. It is as if the lender and the borrower together buy a property and agree that the lender will sell the property to the borrower bit by bit over, say, twenty-five years.

As it is such a serious commitment, I would always advise getting help from someone who understands property and the maths involved. Often the amount you pay over the lifetime of a mortgage can be close to double the cost of the property. Sophie ought to be asking whether the property she wants to buy is really worth *that* amount of money.

Here are four factors that should be borne in mind when considering property investment.

First, consider the rent you would pay for the rest of your life. Mortgages are often more expensive than the rent on a similar-sized property. However, after a twenty-five-year mortgage has been paid, any subsequent property maintenance costs are likely to be much less than the amount of the mortgage. The renter, on the other hand, may have another fifty to sixty years to live, and that is a long time to pay rent with nothing to show for it at the end. This is especially true if property prices rise over that time, because rents go up with property prices, whereas the cost of an individual mortgage does not.

Secondly, in the area where you are planning to buy, what is the economy based on? By this I mean, what are the major industries in the area? How is demand for property likely to hold up over the next ten or twenty years? The major factor in house prices, as with everything else, is supply and demand. If the major industry in your area were to shut down, then everyone would want to sell up and leave, and property prices would plummet. You have only to look at the old pit communities for evidence of this. Indeed, this can be applied at a national level too. One only has to look at the value of property in Zimbabwe over the past few years to see how unstable prices can be.

Thirdly, how much can you contribute to the purchase? The smaller the mortgage as a percentage of the whole cost of buying the property, the less risky the mortgage will be for the lender. This will often lead to a cheaper mortgage deal for the borrower.

Finally, we must consider the affordability of the investment. One of the big factors behind the credit crunch was the provision of mortgages to people who could not afford them, on properties that were not worth the value of the mortgage.

Our inclination will always be to borrow as much as we can in order to buy as big as we can. Sophie might want to think about what she needs with regard to property, rather than what she could afford to keep paying now. Mortgages are commitments for the long term, and since our personal circumstances *and* the economy change over time, the long-term affordability of an investment needs to be considered carefully.

In the end, Sophie will need to decide whether or not she can afford to pay the mortgage off in a range of future circumstances. Mortgages are not the same sort of debt as unsecured loans, and, invested well, that money can grow over time. But we have no God-given right to buy property, so Sophie will need to consider whether it is appropriate for her as she seeks to serve God with her whole life.

Perhaps she needs to stop and take stock of where she is right now.

CHAPTER 6

WHERE ARE YOU NOW?

Beckie is terrified by anything her bank sends her. Most of her statements lie unopened for weeks and are then shoved under her mattress so that they can't distress her further. The idea of getting control of her money appeals, but as soon as she starts to think about the size of the task, she gives up.

Where is she supposed to start? And what if she finds things that she needs to change? She knows that eventually she will need to change, start planning for the future and get control of her giving and spending, but she just can't face doing that today. What would you do if you were Beckie?

Where are you going?

Imagine that you decide to go on holiday. You want to visit family in Cape Town. The question now is: how do you get there? The answer depends on where you are starting your journey from. Right now I am on a train at Wigan. The answer would be different for you, unless you were on the same train as me. In fact, the answer might be *very* different. After all,

I would need to get the train to the airport and then fly. But if you lived in Port Elizabeth, then you would probably drive.

Planning any journey requires knowing where we are travelling from (or it did before GPS), as well as our destination. This chapter is about helping us to understand our starting point, so that we can plan how to get to our desired destination.

A life less ordinary

We have seen that our goal should be a life lived for God now, as we wait for Jesus to return and inaugurate the new creation. Jesus tells us that, in order to gain eternity, we have to give up our right to rule our life, to be willing to go anywhere and do anything for Jesus, to serve everyone in his name (Mark 8:34–38). And the question we need to ask is: are we living that life?

I am certain that we will all know instantly that we have not lived wholeheartedly for God. The section of Mark mentioned above is all about being completely committed to following Jesus' example of selfless sacrificial service of others. Jesus warns us to do absolutely everything we can to give ourselves in the service of others, because it is the last who will be first (Mark 10:31). However, at least one aim of the section is to show us that we can't do this ourselves. We will never serve God perfectly. Only Jesus ever did that, which is one reason why we need to remember that he died in our place (Mark 10:45). But Mark wants to motivate us to give ourselves to serving Jesus in his world, *even though we can't do it perfectly*.

Breaking it down

If you read the little biopic at the start of the chapter and thought, 'That sounds like me', then I hope that this chapter will be especially useful to you. Knowing where to begin in getting to grips with our finances is the hardest part. That is why the first thing I want to do is introduce you to the way I divide up expenditure into categories. I find this helpful for two reasons. The first is simply that thinking about all of our money at once is daunting. If you were to list all the different things you spend money on, that list might easily reach fifty to one hundred items. The more detailed you make it, the longer and the more unwieldy it becomes. Dividing it up means that each list is much shorter and easier to grasp.

The second reason why categories are helpful is that the spending in each one behaves slightly differently, so we need to *think* about them a little differently. Trying to hold on to a variety of expenses when some occur regularly and others annually, some are random and others fixed by contract, can be very confusing indeed. Also, the way in which we apply our biblical principles is slightly different depending on which category we are looking at. (Each category applies of course to specific priorities that we saw in chapter 4.)

I will mention many different types of expenditure in each category. These allocations are not set in stone, and you can move them about. And I won't give a complete list that you have to stick to. These are merely examples, a steer in a direction that I think is helpful, so please do move items around if you think that they ought to be moved.

We're going to think about spending under five headings: fixed necessary expenditure, flexible necessary expenditure, long-term financial planning, giving and variable discretionary expenditure.

1. Fixed necessary expenditure

What is it?
God has promised to provide what is needed for us to survive. The first two categories above cover the expenditure we need in order to have a roof over our heads, food on the table and

clothes to wear. You might say that they meet the first two priorities, namely what is needed for us and for our family.

Under fixed necessary expenditure we can list those items that are fairly predictable from month to month, and which we cannot change to any great degree in the short term.

For most people, this category accounts for quite a large proportion of our monthly outgoings. This is because it includes all regular property-related costs. In order to have a home, most of us will need to pay rent or a mortgage. We also need to pay local government taxes, such as council tax in the UK, and for gas, electricity and water too. Then we will have property insurance. We can't get away from paying for such things if we want to have any kind of normal life.

In this category I would also add fixed costs that relate to earning money to pay the bills. So, for example, if you pay for a rail season ticket or if you drive to work, you incur costs that are inescapable if you are to continue to be employable. And because the journey will be the same most weeks, and prices tend not to change too much, there will be a fixed and predictable cost. You can't avoid it. You just have to pay it.

How does it behave?
It is fair to say that, the majority of the time, changes to the above costs are fairly predictable. Whether your rent will go up next year and by how much can be sorted out months before the rent review comes into force. The same will be true if there is a change in our personal circumstances, such as getting married, having children, offspring leaving home or a new job location. Such changes can make a big difference to what we spend in this 'fixed' category, and the costs just have to be paid because they are necessary to sustain life. But at the same time we do get some warning about these changes and this gives us time to prepare for them.

Many of the changes listed above can make an enormous difference to our outgoings, so it is worth pausing from time to time to ask if our circumstances will change in the coming year and whether or not this will require us to adjust our spending. This will be an important consideration when we come to assess where we are *at present* (at the end of the chapter).

For example, if we are a couple expecting a baby, do we now need to upgrade our house? And can we afford to, given the financial commitment we are making in having a child or children? We need to keep remembering that God is committed to giving us what is *needed*, not what is *wanted*.

It is also worth taking some time to manage our costs. Are we currently with the most competitive mobile phone, internet, gas or electricity provider? By researching these areas and others, we can save hundreds of pounds per year in a relatively short space of time. Of course, the cheapest financial cost may have other costs attached to it, such as environmental or child-labour costs. We will want to consider finances only as part of a wider pool of ethical concerns, as our conscience guides us, when determining where we buy goods and services.

2. Flexible necessary expenditure

As with the first category, we are interested here in what is needed, as we consider our family's spiritual as well as physical needs. We are thinking about costs that can change from month to month, and which as a consequence must be more closely controlled. For that reason, I personally try to monitor our family's costs in this category every couple of months, to ensure that we are not overspending in this area. As I've found out, it is all too easy to spend far more than is needed.

A slightly embarrassing example

When I first sat down to work out my own finances, I discovered something quite disturbing. I was spending about £600 per month on food – at the supermarket, at the takeaway, on nights out with friends, on food consumption generally. I halved that in the following month. As soon as I realized what I was doing, I was able to change. I proved in one month that we can spend much more than we *need* to on things that are *necessary* for us, for not all money spent on food, clothes and so forth is needed, even though some of it clearly is.

I'm not including in this category the clothing or food (for example) that is not essential. I will allow for that under variable discretionary expenditure, with a line for non-work clothing and another for socializing. This is not to suggest that we *shouldn't* spend that money. Indeed, we will spend some for very good relational reasons, but such clothing and food are not needed in order to survive.

All you need is . . .

By the time you have established a sensible level of spending for this category, you will have worked out what it actually costs you to live. And basically we need to be flexible about everything else that follows. I mustn't become wedded to a lifestyle that forces me to turn unnecessary things into needs. By doing that, I am serving me rather than Jesus.

Indeed, seeing that we can live much more cheaply than we had realized has two additional benefits. The first is peace of mind (1 Timothy 6:8). If you find that you can survive on, say, half your income, it gives you a perspective that helps you not to worry about finance

The second is that it has real benefits when we come to planning for the future.

3. Long-term financial planning

Some years ago I visited a financial advisor. I was studying financial advice as part of my professional training, and, as he was advising a friend of mine, I got a free consultation.

Income over time
One of the most useful things he showed me was that our income and our outgoings don't tend to follow the same pattern. Let us consider income, first of all. For most people, income during our employed life looks something like this:

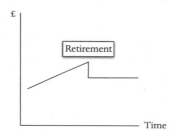

For some people, the income line will go up in steps, for others in a smooth line. For some, the gradient will be shallow, for others steep. But, for most of us, it's the case that when we retire our income will drop from the highest it has ever been to whatever we have set aside for our retirement.

The point that the advisor made was that, without making reasonable provision, our income from retirement will be close to nil. And that would be OK if we could live on nothing. But that isn't the way life works. And given that we might live for thirty years after we retire, we need to realize that this is a large part of our life left unfunded. Let's consider our outgoings.

Expenditure over time
Life's expenditure follows a curve. When we are young and have little responsibility, life is relatively cheap. But suppose we get married and have a family. In a relatively short time, we might move from two incomes and lots of money to one income, a

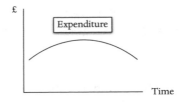

family of four and money being very tight. And it doesn't get any easier as we pay a mortgage on a larger house for the growing family, fork out for our kids' university education, and so on.

When the kids leave home, the mortgage is paid off and life seems easy again. Even on one income life is good, the outgoings are lower, and it is like being twenty-three again. And it becomes easy, under all the temporary costs, to commit to a lifestyle that is totally unsustainable into retirement.

It wouldn't be hard to get used to the lifestyle afforded by a decent salary as we approach retirement. But then to lose our income and find we have no provision put by to live on would be disastrous.

Knowing how little it is possible to live on (categories 1 and 2) allows us to set a minimum level of retirement provision, without which we cannot survive. It is safest not to assume that the state pension will be very significant. We need to make provision for ourselves, provision that will allow us to live reasonably and so not burden the church as we seek to serve God in retirement.

Wider responsibilities

Yet the considerations here go well beyond *us*. As we saw in chapter 4, our primary responsibility once our needs have been met is to ensure that our families, in a reasonably wide sense, have what is necessary for them too. Remember that we have a responsibility to meet genuine needs. And that is all. We are obliged to make sure that our parents, children and so forth have somewhere to live and food on their tables. To put it another way, we need to make sure that they can cover *their* fixed and flexible necessary expenditure. Long-term planning is about providing for us and our family into the distant future.

Consider our expenditure diagram again. Let us imagine that we have both dependent parents and children. The diagram might look like this for us:

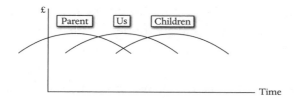

Consider the line representing us. At the beginning of our own parenting, we may find our parents retiring and needing our financial support. At some point, our parents will cease to need our help (though the timing of this is obviously unpredictable), but at the same time the cost of raising children will be growing substantially. By the time they are self-sufficient, we may have little time left to provide for ourselves.

It is, therefore, often necessary to look after our dependants, as well as providing for our own future at the same time. I would like to suggest that it makes good sense to begin making provision for all dependent relatives as soon as we realize that there may be a need.

Planning
Though we will consider this further in later chapters, it's useful to begin to think about it now. Here are a few questions that might help you to make a brief assessment of where you stand:

a) Which of the following best describes you?
   'I earn more than I need.'
   'I spend more than I earn.'
   'I desire more than I can spend.'

How is my answer to a) likely to shape my income and expenditure curves over time?

b) What are my God-given responsibilities? For whom am I going to be responsible during my lifetime? Do I know what that is likely to mean? What are the income and expenditure curves likely to look like for my dependants?

c) What are the likely big costs over the next five to ten years for which it would be wise to save? How can I begin to make provision for them now?

d) What are the likely big costs in the longer term? How can I begin to make provision for those now?

As we consider these questions, let's begin to make a plan. List all the things that you will need to provide for and how much they will *realistically* cost, and work out how to provide for them over the intervening months and years. If you will need to replace your car in five years' time, can you begin to save up now so that you can pay cash rather than buy on credit?

Even as we plan, though, we remember that our heart is deceitful. We only need to provide for that which is necessary. To that end, it is worth setting a maximum level for our savings, and for any retirement provision. Once we know we will be able to care for ourselves and our dependants, it is greed rather than godliness that is driving us to continue to save.

4. Giving

There is nothing in the New Testament that tells us all we would like to know about giving. Often this means that we think we can do what we like, and often as a consequence we don't do very much.

There is some disagreement about how we ought to give, how much and to what. Some will argue that we live in the age of the Spirit and should therefore give as we feel led. I want to agree with that. And yet . . .

The evidence of the Western church

I would love to leave it to how the Spirit guides us. However, the evidence is pretty strongly against that course of action.[1]

For example, Craig Blomberg points out that the average American gives between 1.6% and 2.16% of their income to charity: 'Christians do only slightly better, averaging somewhere around 2.4% of the national per capita income.'[2] In other words, the difference the Holy Spirit makes in 'leading people to give' over and above their pagan neighbours is minimal.

Randy Alcorn observes that 'one study showed that American households with incomes under $10,000 (about £6,000) gave 5.5% of their income to charities, whereas those earning more than $100,000 (about £60,000) gave 2.9%.'[3] He further notes that 'it's a sad statistic that four out of ten church attenders give nothing, and another two or three out of ten give next to nothing'.[4]

I doubt that the statistics would be much different in the UK, though I have not found any parallel studies to prove this.

The simple point is that when there is a rule – the tithe (meaning tenth) – then we are clear about our responsibilities. As soon as we remove the rule, the Christian response seems to be to give as little as our sinful consciences are willing to allow. It is for this reason that Randy Alcorn recommends thinking of tithing as training wheels to get you going. Start at 10% of income, and then ramp up your giving from there, removing the stabilizers.

Joyful, sacrificial giving
Minimal giving is so different from the image Paul gives us in 2 Corinthians 8:1–7:

> **We want you to know, brothers, about the grace of God that has been given among the churches of Macedonia, for in a severe test of affliction, their abundance of joy and their extreme poverty have overflowed in a wealth of generosity on their part. For they gave according to their means, as I can testify, and beyond their means, of their own free will, begging us earnestly for the favour of taking part in the relief of the saints – and this, not as we expected, but they gave themselves first to the Lord and then by the will of God to us. Accordingly, we urged Titus that as he had started, so he should complete among you this act of grace. But as you excel in everything – in faith, in speech, in knowledge, in all earnestness, and in our love for you – see that you excel in this act of grace also.**

It would be easy to give little, relative to our income, and be joyful. It would also be easy to give a great deal and be miserable, giving out of some sense of obligation. But true Christian giving, says Paul, is modelled for us by the Macedonian church: both joyful *and* sacrificial.

You can see their generosity in verse 3, where Paul tells us that they gave beyond their means, and you can see in verse 2 that it was out of their 'abundance of joy' that they gave.

Indeed, they weren't just willing to give – can't you just see them on their knees, pleading with Paul to take the money they were offering?

And Paul is encouraging the Corinthians to copy this model, to 'excel in this act of grace also'. It won't be easy, says Paul. It takes discipline, just like everything truly Christian about us. It flows from our regenerate heart and not from our natural flesh. It flows out of a love for their fellow Christians that goes beyond any desire they have to keep the money for themselves.

Means-tested giving

Paul goes on to say that giving is to be according to our means: 'If the readiness is there, it is acceptable according to what a person has, not according to what he does not have' (verse 12). Paul doesn't set a percentage, but a much more exacting standard. The New Testament model is one of fairness. For some people, giving a tenth would be cheap and easy; for others it would be just impossible.

> *For some people, giving a tenth would be cheap and easy; for others it would be just impossible.*

We see the same thing in Mark 12:41–44. A widow comes to the temple and puts two little coins in the offering. Next to her are the wealthy, who put in their 10%. Jesus commends which of them? 'For they all contributed out of their abundance, but she out of her poverty has put in everything she had, all she had to live on.'

At one and the same time, the New Testament seems to set aside the tithe *and* raise the bar for Christian behaviour. And it all makes sense, since we have the Spirit of Christ empowering us to be generous and joyful.

A better way to think of giving percentages would be this: take your income and subtract tax and the *necessary* costs of living, leaving what is called your 'disposable income'. Now what proportion of that will you give? Consider this example: Jack earns £10,000 and Jill earns £1 million. The cost of necessities is around £8,000 in each case. For Jack to give 10% of his total income would be genuinely sacrificial as it takes away 50% of his disposable income. For Jill to give only £100,000 would be negligible. On the one hand, she might feel really generous and therefore godly, and yet on the other hand she would be keeping much more for herself. The New Testament raises the bar for us and calls us to make our giving genuinely costly.

Deliberate giving

Finally, Paul seems to suggest that we need to be deliberate or our giving will just not happen. The Corinthians had made a commitment to Paul to raise funds for his appeal for the starving saints. But now, a year on, he is worried that he will arrive in Corinth to find that they have nothing for him. So he sends Titus on ahead.

He says:

I thought it necessary to urge the brothers to go on ahead to you and arrange in advance for the gift you have promised, so that it may be ready as a willing gift, not as an exaction. (2 Corinthians 9:5)

Paul doesn't want to force them, but at the same time he understands that good intentions don't get you anywhere unless you act. So he encourages them to put money aside for the collection.

I understand that our situation is different today: we are not usually fund-raising for the relief of the saints specifically. Yet the principle of making a commitment and then endeavouring to stick to it seems to be a prudent one. That is why I have put 'giving' as my fourth category, for we need to make sure that this commitment comes ahead of all our non-necessary expenditure. By this I don't mean that we give everything away. There are, as we've acknowledged, often really good reasons to spend time and money on other things. Nevertheless, if we want to be controlled by God's priorities, then 'giving' needs to come here.

Imagine deciding where to go on holiday first and then deciding what to give out of the money left over. The danger is that you spend everything on your holiday and then have nothing left to give, even if you did have a great holiday. What if we had committed our giving first and then decided what to do about holidays from the balance? That would certainly mean a cheaper holiday. But much better giving.

I suggest dividing giving into two parts. The first is giving that we commit to in advance, which comes under category 4. The second, which I won't say anything else about, is any giving that we will want to make out of our remaining income, as and when the need arises. It is entirely right for us, like the Macedonian Christians, to be willing spontaneously to meet needs as they arise and as we feel led.

The bulk of our giving will come here in category 4. But, first, how much should I give and, secondly, where should that giving go?

How much?

What I suggest is that you decide on a percentage of your gross (before-tax[5]) income. The principle from Paul is that this ought to be an amount that we can give joyfully but also sacrificially. That is to say, we should be happy to give, motivated by the joy that comes from the gospel (and which runs right through the giving teaching in 2 Corinthians 8 – 9).

We ought to notice that we are giving, and it ought to restrict our lifestyle. If my lifestyle and that of my unbelieving friends look similar, then surely it isn't really costing me anything to give, and I am a lot like the rich people in the temple in Mark 12. We need to consider what we can give, and if that is 5% then that is OK. But if you could give 50% of your income away and don't, then put yourself in the temple before Jesus and ask what he would say of you.

It is helpful here to ask what proportion of my disposable income (everything after essentials) I am giving. This will be a helpful barometer of how rich we actually are and help us to set a realistic target.

When I began my working life, all that I earned went to cover essentials. And it was largely the same for my peers. Therefore my life, including my sacrificial giving, looked much the same as everyone else's. As we all began to get promotions and pay rises, the level of disposable income rose disproportionately quickly for everyone. The point here is that, if we allow our peers to set the standard for what is acceptable, we will quickly give up sacrificial living. The pressure to conform will constantly increase as the gap between our standard of living and that of our peers grows. We must be willing to be set apart from the crowd, to see this as a good thing, and to commit ourselves to it.

Where?

Secondly, we want to decide where to give. Remember that God's priority is that people should hear and believe the gospel. Think back to chapter 5, where we looked at the local and the global church, and their spiritual and physical welfare.

I believe that the most substantial part of our giving ought to go to supporting the ministries that our church is involved with, including missionaries and mission organizations. Thus, we might give as a congregation to para-church mission agencies or to specific churches beyond our own. It is, however, important to remember that the pattern of the New Testament is for the local congregation to hold all our possessions in common (Acts 2:44), and to give together to any needs (2 Corinthians 8 – 9; Acts 6; Philippians 4). The primary agency through which God changes the world is the church, not the individual.

There are exceptions to this, however. I can think of a couple of good friends of mine who moved overseas for work. They trusted the minister of their new church but not the church council, who were largely unconverted. Convinced that they had a responsibility to put the money God had given them into the hands of good stewards, they gave their time to the church and their money to ministries elsewhere.

This is a principle that Randy Alcorn makes generally when he says, 'As stewards, we should invest wisely in eternity. This means we must give intelligently, based on an accurate appraisal of those to whom we entrust God's money . . . we need to do our homework before we give.'[6]

At the same time, we might want to put aside some funds to meet needs within the congregation, either as individuals or (more biblically) to be administered by the church (see Acts 6). This allows the church to meet genuine needs, and also to put surplus funds to ministry use.

It is important to know the organizations and individuals to whom we give. If they are Christian in name only, or they are bad stewards of their resources, then we are complicit before God in their negligence. It is, however, time-consuming to make sure each organization that we support is worthy. Giving to missions and so forth as a congregation means that the whole church can help to ensure that the recipients are worthy. This applies also within our own congregations, as two different givers may have a totally different understanding of what it means to meet the *needs* of individual members.

There are any number of para-church organizations that are worthy of our support and which may already have connections with our churches. Many rely entirely on the generosity of Christians and churches to fund their ministry, but please be aware that not every organization deserves support just because it has a good reputation.

5. Variable discretionary expenditure

This category basically covers everything not described above. It is variable because it could be nil or it could be £1 million (if you *have* £1 million!). It is discretionary because you don't need to spend it in order to survive.

Nevertheless, life is more than survival – we want to serve Jesus with our whole life. We will therefore make decisions that fulfil that purpose, and this will undoubtedly entail spending money. I won't even try to provide a comprehensive list, but a few examples might be useful.

As a family, we are keen to extend the gift of hospitality. To do this, we spend more on food than we otherwise would, but hospitality serves the church, so we do it. Also, every couple of years we fly to Canada to visit my parents. That tends to be quite an expensive holiday, but it is a great way to honour my father and mother, as well as a fun holiday.

In that sense, it is quite necessary to budget some of our money in order to behave in a gospel-minded way.

There will also be those costs that, try as you might, you can't find a good gospel reason for. You might love music and enjoy downloading the latest tracks, or enjoy going to the country for walks. God has given us a beautiful, though broken, world to enjoy, and it can be healthy for us to stop and enjoy it. Indeed, the Bible is full of feasting, festivals and thanksgiving. It would therefore be odd for us to have a Father who celebrates (e.g. Luke 15:23) and a Saviour who has a party the night before he dies, and for their followers not to be full of celebration and thanksgiving too.

Nevertheless, it is easy for us to take 'enjoying creation' to extreme levels, and I want us to realize that, if we are going to cut our coat according to our cloth, then this is the area in which we will need to exercise most control. We are not ascetics, but we are not materialists either.

My point here is that items in this category may not be needed for survival, but could well be essential for us to live a purposeful life. It can, however, be hard to distinguish between the two, and so I want to encourage us to ask the question: 'In the light of eternity, how important is this?' and be willing to set spending limits according to the answer.

Where are you now?

Let's pause here and get practical. As far as possible, I have tried to follow biblical principles in creating the divisions we have just seen. We have looked at providing for ourselves, our families, our churches and the wider global church. We've seen that everything else ought to be God-directed. Let us think through a few questions that might help us to assess where we are.

Do you agree with the last couple of chapters?

Have I got this wrong? If you don't agree with me, then it is important for me to ask a further question: Do you disagree with the theology or with the way I have applied the theology? This is important, because it tells me whether your disagreement is with me or with God. If you don't like my structure for dealing with money, then feel free to change it to suit your needs. If your disagreement is with God, then it is you who will need to change, not him.

If you have found this book helpful so far, then it is worth pausing and thinking about what might need to change.

What does your life look like?

Why not write out the five category headings on a piece of paper? Under each one, write down the things on which you spend money, as I have described them. Some items will be hard to place: for example, some shoes you will need to buy; others you will just buy because you like shoes. It is OK to split clothing between two categories in this way.

Against each item under each category, write down what you think you spend in a month. You might also like to have a couple of lines at the top for sources of income as well. The point is to see whether or not we really do know what we spend, and where. As I have said already, when I first went through this process I was stunned at what I spent in some categories. Be honest and don't start by looking through your bank statements. How well do you really know what you spend, and where? We will come back to this information shortly.

Deceptive hearts

My aim here is to expose our hearts so that we will not trust them. In Jeremiah 17:9 we are told:

> **The heart is deceitful above all things, and desperately sick; who can understand it?**

We cannot trust our own instincts, our sense of what we are doing, because our hearts lie to us. Jesus makes the same point in Mark 7:20–23 when, among a long list of evils that come out of the heart, he mentions deceit. This leads us to our fourth biblical principle:

Bible principle 4:
The heart is deceitful above all things, so don't trust it

By writing down what we think we spend, we are really articulating what our own senses tell us, what our hearts as our 'control centre' really believe. This will give us a marker against which we can measure the truth. Our hearts carry some false and some true information. We cannot trust our sense of what we do with money to guide us in our decision-making. What we really need is the truth, because knowledge is the key to wise decisions.

Testing the theory

My challenge to you at the end of this chapter is to keep records for at least a month, or preferably two. Write down everything you spend under each category. Make the records as detailed as you can because the numbers carry information about your spending habits. (I always encourage people to carry around a note book and just write down everything that you spend.) This shouldn't be too onerous, and will give you a good basis upon which you can make plans for the future (as we will see in chapter 8).

At the end of the month, tot up what you have spent in each category and compare this with the initial impressions that you wrote down earlier. Many items will be similar, because your senses are not dead, but it is important to notice the *big* differences. It is here that your heart is deceiving you.

And please, you mustn't cheat. The idea is that you will live your life normally while doing this exercise. It will be natural that, because you are writing down everything, you will become more conscious of some items. You might even feel guilty as you begin to see how much you are spending on certain things. This is normal. Nevertheless, if you don't live naturally during this month or so, you won't get a true picture of what you spend in everyday life. If that happens, the only person you are kidding is yourself.

So what does my life look like?

So far we have seen that God wants to get us, and everyone else, to the new creation through faith in Jesus. Living for the new creation means living with God in charge, and *that* means living with his priorities.

When you look at the numbers that describe your life for the past month or two, do they describe that sort of life? Are you living a God-centred or a self-centred life?

> *Are you living a God-centred or a self-centred life?*

The chances are that you are somewhere in between. None of us lives for God perfectly, nor will any Christian be completely compromised. But in the big areas, we need to be honest: are our big decisions being governed by God and his purposes, or by our own?

Starting to plan

Whatever the answer, we can repent of all past wrongs and start to make decisions that honour God. To help us all to do that, I am going to ask us to draw what our life currently looks like and what we would like it to look like in order to honour God more. It will help us to have a target.

For most of us, diagrams are really helpful for getting an impression of what the numbers mean. So, using the diagram on page 107 as an example, try drawing your own.

The idea is to draw a U-shaped graph. On the left-hand axis, you put your gross annual income. On the right-hand axis, put the equivalent hours worked. So, in my diagram, the person who works a typical year would earn roughly £25,000 and work about 2,100 hours to earn it.[7] Each shaded area represents the amount of your earnings that you spend on that category, and the equivalent hours you spend earning that money.

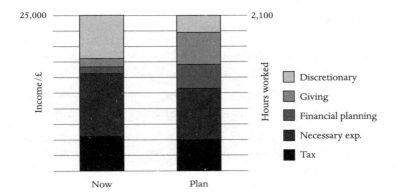

Now divide the left-hand column between the five boxes, based on how you think you spend your money. In the example above, roughly the first £6,000 (or 504 hours) goes to the tax man and the next £10,000 (840 hours) goes on necessary expenditure. Only about £2,500 (210 hours) is split between financial planning and giving, with the remaining £6,500 (546 hours) being spent on discretionary items. What does the left column look like for you?

On the right-hand column, redraw the diagram for how you would like your life to look. Could you reduce your taxes by giving tax-efficiently? Could you save more? Could you give more? How could you reorder your life to reflect God's priorities? What sort of life do you want to live?

The rest of this book is about helping you to get there.

Study questions:

1. What do you find most helpful about the divisions in this chapter? What do you find least helpful? Why?
2. What big differences did you find between what you thought you would spend and what you actually spent?
3. What are the big changes you would like to make over time?

CHAPTER 7

INVESTING IN YOUR FUTURE

From time to time, most of us will be in a position to decide to train for our work. Whether it be work experience, an apprenticeship, going to university or professional training, whether it be straight out of school, after university or in our forties, the decision will involve committing time and probably money (either spent or foregone earnings) that might otherwise be used elsewhere. How do we come to that decision? Consider the following example.

> Darren is seventeen years old and thinking about going to university. Most of his friends are being encouraged to do so, and he likes the idea of moving away from home and being independent. However, Darren is concerned about the wisdom of going to university. He isn't sure what he wants to do afterwards, and the cost is very high (he estimates about £30,000 to study and £60,000 in lost earnings over three years). He knows that his parents can't afford to fund his whole education. Should he go and incur debt for an education that he might not afterwards need? Could the money his parents spend be better used for Christ's work? In fact, what is an education really worth?

Without wanting to suggest that money is the only deciding factor (which it certainly isn't), we must recognize that it is indeed a big factor. For some it is prohibitive. And even if you can afford it, the question is: should you go? It is absolutely right to want to weigh the benefits against the obvious costs and ask whether it is actually worth it.

To be a student or not to be a student . . .

There is a range of good reasons to go to university. There is the obvious academic benefit of expanding one's mind in a field of study. There are the social benefits of interacting with like-minded, or indeed totally *un*like-minded, individuals in a safe environment. There are ministry opportunities for Christians among people willing to explore the meaning of life. All good reasons.

Yet I want to argue that one of the primary reasons for going to university is economic.

We saw in chapter 3 that time = money × (skills + energy). That is, as a student we will exchange time and effort, and forego earnings from being employed for a number of years, in order to invest in our employability. We will go to university to invest in skills that qualify us for a particular field of employment that might otherwise be closed to us.

So further education is an investment in our own future. We study because, at the end of that study, either we are allowed to do a job we would otherwise be disqualified from, such as being a doctor, or we are more valuable to an employer, and so are paid more (or indeed both).

It is therefore right that Darren should ask, 'Why do I want to be a student?' Given the person that I am, with the skills God has given me, is going to university the wisest path, the best place to use my time and energy? Darren isn't sure of the answer. It might be wise for him to take a gap year and think about his options, exploring various alternative careers. Once he has some idea about what he wants to do, it is wise to ask whether he could enter that field without a degree.

And if the answer is yes (and for many it will be), then the question ought to be: 'Is it worth it for me to go?' If he is not going to gain the skills that compensate for the cost, then, all other things being equal,[1] it isn't worth going.

University education costs many thousands of pounds that could be used for gospel causes. Even if Darren's parents *could* afford to fund his study, should they do so?

Having made the decision to go, the next question we might ask is . . .

Who is responsible for paying?
We saw earlier that the nuclear family has a responsibility for its dependants. Sending someone to university is something that the whole family ought to agree on, and the whole family ought to be involved in supporting the student.

As far as possible, the family ought to aim for the student not to get into debt. Clearly, this is not something that will be possible for every family, nor will every family recognize that responsibility. But even though debt may be required, many will perceive that the benefits of going to university are worth the investment.

The cost of an education can of course vary dramatically. It can depend on the lifestyle of the student, and on where the student lives and studies. As such, a budget ought to be drawn up by the family, to which both the student and the family are committed, as part of the process of training the student to be self-supporting. (More about this in chapter 9.)

Let us assume for the sake of argument that some debt is required.

How do we view student debt?

Student debt is so common, and so often necessary, that for many the decision to get into debt is made instinctively. Without proper consideration, however, the decision defaults to getting whatever we can rather than what we need. This is a major error. There is a great difference between £5,000 of debt and £15,000. Rather than taking as much as is available, the Christian student will want to limit debt to what is needed in order to live.

As in a business or property investment, the more the education costs, the greater the return needed. If the cost of your education is going to be £50,000, then however it is funded, you have to be sure of a commensurate return. Clearly, an education that costs £10,000, with the student living at home, for example, would be a different matter altogether.

Once a student is living in debt, I often hear the question, 'Should I give to my church?' This is a fair question, because it can often feel as if it is not our money to give, and since debt is not something to get into lightly, it makes little sense to get into even *more* debt by giving to the church.

There are two issues here.

The first is that debt is debt and should therefore be limited. We get into debt only in order to cover necessities. We have only a very little frivolous spending (on beer, clothes, music, etc.). Because of that, I want to suggest that giving is not required. I think the Bible rates our responsibility to our families ahead of giving, so our attempts not to get into debt should be sufficient.

Even here, however, if we are willing to sacrifice something we think of as necessary, perhaps part of a meal, we will emulate the Macedonians in 2 Corinthians 8 by giving beyond our means. Such giving benefits us now as it makes us more God-centred, and sets important patterns for our future discipleship.

Secondly, we could consider debt as an advance against our future income. We will be paid more, and it is only *as* we are paid more that the debt will need to be repaid (though the level of income at which the debt needs to be repaid is roughly 40% *below* the national earnings average, so almost every student will have to pay it back). By recognizing that we are spending money we will earn in the future, rather than thinking of it as debt, we behave as though our future job were providing a similar lifestyle while studying to that which we hope to enjoy after university.

I take it that, in practice, this is how most students live. Socializing, clothes shopping and so forth are part of student life because they are part of life generally. However, if we choose to behave like this, then I believe there is no place for saying, 'I can't give money to the church because it is not my money.' In practice, we are already denying that by our behaviour in these other areas.

When it comes to being a student, our attitude should be one of obedience to God, and therefore a desire to develop good habits of financial management.

Making a plan

So what we are advising Darren to do is think through the costs and benefits of a university education, and consider the alternative routes to his chosen career. It might be entirely legitimate to take a year or two to investigate career paths. Many people leave university and spend years trying to work out what they want to do, but only *after* incurring a lot of debt. Darren would be wise to find out what he really wants to do *before* committing three years or more to a course that has no definite purpose.

It's well worth taking time out to make a plan, as the alternative can be very costly. The rest of this book is about helping you to make such a plan, so we'll take a look next at one area where this really affects our decision-making.

CHAPTER 8

I LOVE IT WHEN A PLAN COMES TOGETHER

Andy has a busy life. He is involved in the church youth group, works long hours, has two cats and is enjoying a burgeoning relationship with Loïs. He is committed to living for Jesus, but for a long time has feared that getting to grips with his money will take too much time away from other important areas.

However, Andy recently read 2 Corinthians 8 – 9 and was convinced that the Bible seems to take the issue of financial godliness seriously. Andy has asked John, an accountant at church, to help him to gain control of his finances. Andy has made a list of all his spending for the last two months, and, though he is slightly embarrassed about a few things, he knows that failure to plan for the next year will also mean that he will fail to change.

The story so far . . .

In the 1987 movie *Wall Street*, the banker Gordon Gekko coined the phrase 'Greed is good.' It's a line that resonated with baby-boomers in the 1980s. And I think it still resonates with us today, as we are living in a culture that has largely abandoned God and forgotten his promises, and thus has no hope for the future, which of course means that people live for the present.

Let's do a quick recap. Our whole economic system is built on this supposed need to own everything now, and that a Christian can buy into that philosophy every bit as much as the next person. Yet God does exist, and he has promised us a perfect new creation where all the longings of this life will find their ultimate satisfaction.

Our second Bible principle was, 'Everything belongs to God', including us and the money he has entrusted to us. We are stewards, not owners. It isn't for us to decide what to do with God's things. He has told us plainly what he thinks is important, and our job is to align ourselves with his will.

This is difficult, though, because our hearts deceive us. Too often we live to please ourselves. So how can we change the way in which we live so that we can rejoice in serving God?

But before we look at the practicalities of change, of making plans and sticking to them, let's see where the power to change and the joy in change come from.

The power for change

In the New Testament, Paul knows only too well the conflict between living God's way and living our own way. In Galatians 5, he is addressing the question of how we ought to live:

> **I say, walk by the Spirit, and you will not gratify the desires of the flesh. For the desires of the flesh are against the Spirit, and the desires of the Spirit are against the flesh, for these are opposed to each other, to keep you from doing the things you want to do. But if you are led by the Spirit, you are not under the law. Now the works of the flesh are evident: sexual immorality, impurity, sensuality, idolatry, sorcery,**

enmity, strife, jealousy, fits of anger, rivalries, dissensions, divisions, envy, drunkenness, orgies, and things like these. I warn you, as I warned you before, that those who do such things will not inherit the kingdom of God. But the fruit of the Spirit is love, joy, peace, patience, kindness, goodness, faithfulness, gentleness, self-control; against such things there is no law. And those who belong to Christ Jesus have crucified the flesh with its passions and desires.

In Paul's view, if we are Christians, we have a conflict going on within us. 'Flesh' is Paul's word for everything worldly: our sinful nature and all our desires to live apart from God's will. In the list of 'works of the flesh' from verse 19, Paul isn't giving us a comprehensive list of evils, but already we can see many that we have encountered before: idolatry, jealousy, rivalry and envy. This is what the world is like, says Paul. The end for such people is to be cut off from God for eternity (verse 21).

But, says Paul, if you are a Christian then you have a second set of desires at work in you: desires that come from God himself by his Spirit. That is where the conflict of verse 17 comes from. We have the world living in our flesh and desiring us to do anything that opposes God. But we also have the Spirit, who opposes our rebellion and seeks for us to display the fruit of being in the kingdom. It is in our new nature as Christians to be loving, joyful, patient, and so on.

Just as the fruit of a tree doesn't appear the minute you plant the sapling, so Christian fruit takes time to mature. Yet the promise for the Christian is that change will happen by the power of the Holy Spirit. And it happens gradually, as we make the daily choice to live for God and not for our flesh.

The Spirit's power enables us to change joyfully as we become more like Jesus. What this looks like in practice is a daily decision to live for Jesus, something which brings us neatly to the source of joy.

A matter of love and hate

But the Holy Spirit doesn't just give us power to change. The new desires within us are based on, and rooted in, the gospel, and it is through the gospel that we are changed. As we understand that Jesus died to reconcile us to God, to bring us into his family so that we can call him Father, as we understand our new relationship to the church, and as we look forward to our new future, so we become more like Jesus. As the Holy Spirit applies the message of Jesus to our hearts, so he gives us joy in the gospel, and this changes our loves and hates.

We might say, then, that change is only possible to the extent that we have understood the gospel as it applies to us.

The first church

We have already seen the effects of the gospel on the early church in Acts 2, how they shared all they had with one another and raised funds for famine relief when believers elsewhere were in need, and we saw that all aspects of the fellowship of that early church were rooted in the teaching of the gospel. As the apostles unfolded the truth about Jesus, the church naturally desired to live according to its new status as a family.

The one church

We have also seen how this works at a global level. The local church is to love the international church, regardless of how different that church is from our own. Paul used his experience of going on a fund-raising missionary journey in Acts 11, and the exceptional generosity of the Macedonian church, to encourage the Corinthians, and, by extension, us, to give generously, as our Father has done.

Real change of heart

Change must happen because God has changed the things that we love, so that we now love to honour him.

But change in the heart, real change from new loves and new desires, will happen only if we are converted and continue to believe the gospel. As we make it our habit to listen to God's word, read the Bible and ask God to speak to us, so we will be changed organically, just as the fruit grows on a tree as we water and care for it.

Christians have the resources to change, to live generously, because we believe in a generous God who has *already* secured access for us to the place of perfect blessing. There is simply nothing in this life that can come close to what God has secured by the death and resurrection of Jesus.

This leads us to our fifth Bible principle:

> **Bible principle 5:**
> Real change flows from
> a firm grasp of the gospel,
> by the Spirit

The first time I read that I had to love Jesus more than my parents, I was nineteen and I cried shamelessly. I couldn't see how it could be done. I was a new Christian and I couldn't see how Jesus had done more for me than my parents had done. I wanted to please them more than him because they seemed more worthy.

But as I began to grasp the gospel – the depth of my sin, the love of Jesus in leaving glory to die for me while I was still his enemy, and the great rewards he had won for me – I realized that it was Jesus alone who was worthy of my devotion.

Getting down to the nitty-gritty

Having made sure of our motives, we need to think through how we are going to change. The accountant's word for this is 'budget' (if you don't like this word, then stick to 'plan'!).

In order to make an annual budget, we need to bear two things in mind.

First, all the change that we would like to make may not be possible in a year. It depends on how big it is and how much of a lifestyle adjustment is needed. The objective with a budget is to make it achievable.

Secondly, we need to bear in mind the longer term. We will need to think about the big changes that will happen in five, ten, twenty years' time, so that we can plan this year accordingly. Are there events in the future that, if your life were to go according to your plan, you ought to provide for now? As our plans are always subject to change, there is no need to go into very great detail for events that are, say, twenty years away. Nevertheless, some careful planning now will mitigate the impact of significant future events.

It is worth noting that both the longer-term plans and the single-year budget are subject to change at any time. I had just completed the budget for 2007/8 when we found out that my wife was pregnant. Suddenly a number of important factors (such as income, cost of food, etc.) needed to change. Big life events are not always predictable. Having a longer-term plan in mind, into which our annual budget fits, allows us to adapt to our new circumstances without losing sight of those plans that remain unaffected.

The benefit of having an eye on the future is obviously particularly important for longer-term financial planning, where decisions about pensions, savings and so forth are made. And having a broad-brush view of the future allows us to make some informed decisions for the coming year.

I believe, however, that real change happens in the nitty-gritty, everyday-life decision-making. To decide, for example, to cut £100 from your food bill each month is admirable. But that will need to be matched by a change in your food-buying habits if it is to be any more than a good intention. If we are going to change, we need to make specific changes to our habits, which will involve making a detailed plan. I have broken the steps of this plan down so that we can think more carefully about the questions we want to ask. I have also provided the table below to illustrate what this might look like. In the interests of space I haven't included every category, but I hope that the shape of the table will help you visualize what you should be aiming to produce.

		Jan	Feb	Mar	Apr	May	Jun	Jul		Total
Fixed nec. exp.	Rent	1,000	1,000	1,000	1,000	1,000	1,000	1,000		12,000
	Council tax	75	75	75	75	75	75	75	Etc.	900
	Electricity	70	70	70	70	70	70	70		840
Fixed nec. exp.	Food	220	210	200	190	180	180	180		2,180
	Travel	70	50	70	60	50	80	80		800
Etc.										
Total		xx	xx	xx	xx	xx	xx	xx		yy

Start as you don't mean to go on

At this point, you may wish to reach for a spreadsheet or equivalent. What we are going to do is map out the next year, assuming that you will change nothing. But before we can really have a go at changing, we need to have a clear idea of what our current habits are.

If you have kept records of your spending for a month or two, then you are already halfway there. These will be the basis for estimating a whole year. If you haven't been doing this, then I suggest that you start now, as it will really help you to plan. On a spreadsheet or a piece of paper, write the next twelve months across the top and your categories down the left-hand side. I always put income at the top and expenses underneath.

Using your records, estimate what you will spend in the next year. It may be easiest to start by filling in every month the same and then going through the categories to think through the following points:

- Are there any one-off items that I have not included, such as holidays?
- Are there particular events, such as Christmas and birthdays, which will predictably break the regular pattern?
- Are there possible events of which it is impossible to predict the timing, such as trips to the optician? (Put the cost of such a trip in *somewhere*.)

Once you have made appropriate changes, you now have your best estimate of what a year in your life looks like in financial terms. The next two steps will help you to change that future in positive ways.

Cash is the key

In any organization, from government to the family home, running out of cash is bad news. It means that we cannot pay our bills and buy our food or indeed any number of other things necessary to sustain life. It forces us into debt and, as many national governments have found out to their detriment, eventually the debts will be called in.

I mention this because we need to understand the flow of cash represented by what we have just drawn up. At the bottom of my schedule, I take the total income for the month and deduct total expenses to get the movement in cash for the month.

Beneath that, I place another line that begins with my initial balance and adds on the movement each month, so that I know how much I will actually have at the end of the month.

Underneath *that*, I always put in another line called *Lowest cash level*. The lowest cash level is the point in the month, usually just before payday, when I have spent money but have not received any. For example, if I were paid £1,000 per month and spent £1,000 per month, then I might be deceived into thinking that everything was fine. But if I am paid at the end of the month, most of the expenditure will occur before I get paid. In other words, I will have a lowest cash level of −£1,000.

So I will need to have £1,000 in the bank at the start of the month in order to be able to remain solvent until the next payday.

Putting a leash on the spending beast

The table can help us to see what we predict our lowest cash level to be for the whole year. Let us say, for example, that we are expecting to have a lowest cash level of −£1,500 in December. We know that our bank doesn't want us to go overdrawn, so we have to make plans now to prevent that. We can do two things here.

First, we can consider those costs that we intend to pay, of which we are in control of the timing. For example, *when* we pay for our holidays is largely in our hands. If we can postpone paying for them until the New Year, for example, then we can smooth our spending and improve our lowest cash position (though the cost of postponing payment of things like holidays can admittedly push up the price if there is a concession for early payment).

The second thing we can do is to make savings by changing our spending habits. We might look through our categories and ask, 'Where could I make savings?' We could cut some expenditure from food, socializing, clothes and any number of other items. It might not need to be a lot, but altogether it could save a lot.

In fact, this is an exercise that we can take one step further as we make our plan to live proactively for Jesus. Before I go there, though, it is worth saying that you will not be able to predict the whole year with very great confidence on the basis of one or two months of spending. We'll come back to reviewing this every month or so (in chapter 11), but at this stage it is worth building into the plan a line for the unexpected, perhaps at £50–£100 per month. The more nervous you are about the accuracy of your budget, the more you will need as a contingency.

What does living for Jesus look like for you?

We have already seen generally what it will look like to have God's priorities. However, I cannot tell you what this will look like in your life specifically. Everyone is different, with varying responsibilities and opportunities, so I cannot simply map my life on to yours and tell you to live this way or that.

However, the next exercise is designed to help us ask: does my spending in each area reflect God's priorities? I suggest that you go through your table line by line and ask what each total says about your personal priorities.

1. Income

The place to begin is with our income. I always assume that predictable increases in income, such as from pay rises, will not happen until we are told about them for certain. It is generally better to assume a worst-case scenario for both income and expenses so that all your surprises are positive ones.

Income sets the limits on what you can spend. If you can live within the boundaries set by your current income, then any pay rises you get will be bonus money to be used as God would direct.

2. Fixed necessary expenses

To a large extent, fixed necessary expenses are already determined. However, it is worth making a couple of observations.

First, you need to make sure that your list is complete. Have you included such one-offs as water rates and home insurance? The nature of fixed necessary expenses is that they tend to be large and unavoidable. Missing something out here could bring a nasty surprise later on in the year. Ask an experienced budgeter to look through your categories to make sure you have everything covered.

Secondly, there may be decisions to make during the year, which may provide an opportunity to save money, such as whether or not to move house (particularly if you are renting).

3. Flexible necessary expenses

Here the question to ask is: are the amounts I am showing 'necessary', or am I building in indulgences too?

4. Longer-term financial planning

For longer-term planning, my advice is to speak to a financial advisor. At the very least, all of us will want to discuss pensions. Beyond that, we may also need to think of the best way of saving to provide for future circumstances, such as dependent relatives. I suggest finding a Christian advisor if possible, perhaps in your church, because he or she is more likely to understand your priorities.

If you have set a sensible level of living costs, then you know what your retirement plans need to cover. As I suggested earlier, if we anticipate major future expenses, including our retirement provision, we can calculate what we ought to put aside from one month to the next. As events come round, we can adjust the amount we need to keep saving, to reflect the reduction in future expenses.

In this area especially, it would be easy to underestimate our needs. Seeking professional advice can help to remove worry and give us peace of mind regarding the plans we are making. Be aware, however, that most professional advisors are paid by the financial institutions whose packages they sell. It therefore makes sense also to have a maximum level of savings and retirement provision in mind before you speak with them.

5. Giving

I suggest that you look at what you are presently giving as a percentage of income and decide how much you want to increase it. A cursory review of your other outgoings will allow you to make an educated guess at how much you could increase your giving before it would truly become sacrificial. I would then encourage you to push that amount a little higher. Not much, perhaps, but enough for it to have an impact on your lifestyle.

Plan to increase your giving at every opportunity. As our disposable income increases over time, with pay rises, it is our standard of giving, not our standard of living, that ought to rise. Just pause and think about the people in your home group at church. How many wage earners are there? Eight? Ten? Imagine if each were able to raise their giving by an average of £2,000 per year. Between you, there is the opportunity to fund a member of staff for your church, or a couple of missionaries for a whole year. Imagine if your whole church did this. Alternatively, imagine what opportunities your church is missing out on because, as a church, you are unwilling to make the lifestyle changes that could mean a massive difference. And what difference could *you* make?

Once you have decided how much to give, decide how you wish to allocate your giving and then set up standing orders with the various organizations that you've chosen. Please, if your government offers tax incentives to charitable givers, such as the Gift Aid scheme in the UK, make sure you fill in all the necessary paperwork to allow you and the charity or church to claim those incentives.

6. Check your bottom line

In both of the last two sections, we are likely to have increased our outgoings. So we need to start making savings elsewhere. By looking at the difference between our income and our outgoings, we are now in a position to see how much we ought to cut out of our budget to make it balance. If we think of it in chapter 3 terms, this is really our marginal money. Some things will be reduced, and some will go altogether. The question is: which things really matter?

Start with the categories that are most important, such as food, and make sure that they are as low as is reasonably possible. Our largest variable outgoings will tend to be on things such as food, socializing, holidays and clothing. We are looking to reduce these to liveable and sensible levels.

Let me illustrate from my own life. When I realized how much I was spending on going out with friends, I decided that it would be cheaper for everyone if I cooked instead. I enjoy cooking, so this wasn't exactly a hardship, and I still got to spend time with friends, which was the reason we socialized. We didn't cut socializing out of our lives, just changed the location.

But consider this: if nine friends and I go out for dinner and spend just £10 per head, that is £100 for the evening. If I do this twice a month for the year, then it amounts to £2,400. Now imagine that I can cook for ten people for about £25. That isn't even trying to be economical. But it saves the group of friends £1,800 in a year. And if we share the cost, then nobody loses out. Each person saves £180.

It is small shifts in thinking like this, across a variety of areas, that will make a big difference in the end.

Could you buy supermarket own brands rather than the more expensive popular brands? Could you set a limit on clothes-buying so that you have to choose between items, rather than buying everything you want? Could you limit how frequently you buy coffee from a coffee shop? Every little step over a year can make a big difference.

You could also think about how you might save money by paying early. By booking your holiday early, you might save a vast proportion of the cost. If you pay for your home or car insurance in instalments, you probably pay about 30% interest on the outstanding balance. By paying a lump sum, you save a considerable amount.

When I left my last paid job to enter our church's voluntary ministry training scheme, our household income halved. My wife commented a few months later that she hadn't really noticed the change in our standard of living. By making a decision to be restrained in a few key areas, we had already made big savings.

7. Contingencies

Despite the best planning in the world, our future is in God's hands, and what happens will not perfectly match our own vision. It is, therefore, a good idea to build a 'worst-case-scenario' fund into the budget.

For our family of four, I put £75 per month into the budget to cover items that I haven't foreseen, or for a number of smaller items that it isn't worth budgeting for specifically. It's not our aim to put a line in the budget for every conceivable item. The process is not designed to be burdensome, just detailed enough to be informative, so I always advise that we put in a single line for miscellaneous items.

Over time you will grow more confident at assessing what needs have their own line in the budget, and how much you should put in under miscellaneous.

If you are married, you may also want to set aside pocket money for each partner. I have found this to be a really useful idea, as it allows my wife and me to spend what we like on ourselves, or each other, without being accountable, within the limits set by our pocket money. So if I want to go for a curry with the boys, or my wife wants a pair of shoes, we have a little flexibility to do this. As long as both partners know what they are expected to spend that money on, then this works quite well. Pocket money also helps to train each member of the family to make the sort of decisions on a small scale that the whole family needs to make on a larger scale.

How do you feel now?

How do you feel now? Intimidated? Happy? Relieved? Horrified? There could be any number of emotions, depending on whether you find numbers easy or hard and whether you are an organized or disorganized sort of person.

In my experience, following this process is never as bad as it sounds, and it always helps people to gain control of their finances. Having said that, it does take time, at least to begin with. Like all disciplines that are spiritually motivated, it can seem odd at first because it is not something we

Think of it as taking up a new sport: you learn the rules and understand the theory, but it takes time for you to adjust on the pitch.

have ever done before. Think of it as taking up a new sport: you learn the rules and understand the theory, but it takes time for you to adjust on the pitch. Over time, the rules and theory become a part of how you play the game; they are the new governing principles of your life in that sport. I think it works the same way with spiritual disciplines: odd to begin with, but through practice they can become second nature.

So why not give this one a go?

Study questions:

1. Do you find yourself rejoicing regularly in the gospel? What might help you to do this more?
2. What do you find most intimidating in this chapter? Do you have a friend who might help you?
3. What changes do you need to make to your spending habits today?

CHAPTER 9

EQUIPPING THE CHURCH

Pete is forty-five years old, a father of three and the pastor of a small church in Hampshire. He has always been pretty good at keeping the family finances in good order, but lately he has been wondering how best to help his children to learn to handle money themselves before they leave home. He has also noticed that the Bible speaks a lot about money, and he is concerned that, out of fear of sounding like a tin-rattling televangelist, he hasn't said enough about money from the pulpit. What should he do?

In many ways, Pete has done the hardest part. As he has already got his own finances under control, whatever he teaches at home or in church will be grounded in years of personally trying to honour God with his money. However, there are still some areas where we could advise.

We all find ourselves in a position of influence in the lives of others – in the house group or friendship circle; in a pastoral setting or in the home. How should we incorporate our new thinking about money into these contexts?

The smallest church

Every parent is a pastor in his or her own home, with a special privilege to go with this responsibility. In 1 Thessalonians, Paul describes his ministry among the Thessalonians as sharing both the gospel and his life (1 Thessalonians 2:8). Any pastor will tell you how hard it is to share his whole life with the entire congregation. But every parent *has* to share his life with his children, for good or ill. What an opportunity!

Living the Christian life in front of our kids is costly, but it does have some real benefits. It is costly because we want to protect them from stressful financial situations, or from 'boring' decisions, and because we don't want to 'get it wrong' in front of them. However, I believe that most kids *want* to feel involved in decision-making and running the house, and that this sort of training is priceless for at least three reasons.

First, and most importantly, modelling the Christian life grounds what we *teach* in what we *do*. It is one thing to tell our kids that they ought to give generously to the church. But they will only understand this properly if we show them what it costs the family to give, and invite them to help us decide how much to give and to what.

Secondly, it fosters a sense of responsibility. Knowing the value of money and the financial situation of the family helps children to have realistic expectations. My cousin tells the story of a friend who complained to her that she didn't know what to get her kids for Christmas that year because they already had everything they wanted. The parents had a policy of spending £700 per Christmas on each child, so by now the children had all the TVs and games consoles they could cope with. That is a really dangerous situation because it tells the child, 'We have all the money in the world, and you can have whatever you want.' Not only is that untrue, it is risky to leave home (eventually) thinking that you can have anything you want without the money running out. Realizing that buying X means foregoing Y is one of the best lessons to teach your kids. It is also useful for them to learn that money needs to be earned, perhaps by doing simple chores around the house.

Remember that we were made to work. It may be dull or painful for us after the fall (in Genesis), but it is something we do for our whole life, even into the new creation. Getting your children to understand the connection between work and rewards now will be an invaluable life lesson later.

Thirdly, there are situations that arise only rarely in life, such as moving home. Perhaps a child might move once or twice while growing up. Each of those occasions is an opportunity to explain how to make decisions about where to live, how much to spend, whether or not to get a mortgage and for how much. These are massive decisions, but decisions that your kids will invariably have to deal with when they are older. What an opportunity to help them to understand the important considerations before they get there!

Keith Tondeur says, 'You need to establish a strategy of independence for your children.'[1] Part of discipling our children is helping them to understand what it takes to make the wisest choices. We need to be creative as we think of how to instil good habits in children from a young age. We can model budgeting as a family and encourage them to do something similar with their pocket money. Teaching them how to save for something important, how to give, and when it is OK to spend on things they want, is a valuable life lesson that, if learned with little as children, will endure when they have much more later on. Our ambition is that, when they leave home, they will be able to cope in the world in every area of their life. Independence doesn't mean that they never come to us for advice, but it does mean that they learn to live within their God-given financial constraints in the course of normal life.

According to Randy Alcorn, 'Children can't learn money management unless they have money to manage and unless that money is earned by their effort. I can't overemphasise this point – parents who shovel out money according to the dictates of the moment are not teaching their children proper stewardship.'[2]

Our question here must be: 'What sort of disciples of Jesus do I want to bring up when it comes to money?' That should control how we raise our children.

Ministry to the church

Money is not a subject that we like to teach on at church, and no wonder. It feels like a very private matter. We are cautious about telling people what we earn in case they become jealous, judgmental or condescending. And congregations don't want to be told to give to the church; nor do pastors want to be seen to be begging.

Even though money is mentioned, on average, twice on every page of Scripture, we can go for months without mentioning it directly at church. It is easy, even in a passage that speaks explicitly about money, to draw a principle for the whole of life rather than press home the financial applications.

Imagine, for example, teaching Mark 10:17–31 on the rich man who refuses to give up his earthly wealth to follow Jesus. It would be easy to say, 'Jesus put his finger on *this man's* idol – but he definitely isn't saying that everyone should give up all their wealth to follow him.'

That would, in a sense, be true. Yet I fear that this would be to empty the passage of its force. The passage does say that if you are not *prepared* to give up what you have to follow Jesus, then your money and possessions are *your* idol, just as they were in the case of the rich man. Jesus demands that we be *willing* to give up everything to follow him, to transfer ownership back to the Lord who made it all.

Jesus was willing to teach on money – often. He knew what a barrier money could be to faith: 'No one can serve two masters, for either he will hate the one and love the other, or he will be devoted to the one and despise the other. You cannot serve God and money' (Matthew 6:24). Here were two possible gods. Which do you choose? Jesus is blunt. So is Paul, in telling us that 'the love of money is a root of all kinds of evils' (1 Timothy 6:10a).

We must remember that the Bible warns us about money, not only because it can be an idol in its own right, but also because it is the path to every other idol. Health, security, privacy, power, fame, sex, self-esteem – all can be bought with a fat wallet.

Not only is the pastor to live out the gospel, but he must present all of God's word to his people (Acts 20:27). It is right that we don't become obsessed with talking about money. Nevertheless, if we are going to lay the balance of Scripture before people, then we will speak of it more often than we tend to do now.

Whether at home with children or in the church, we do well not to hold back, but to teach others about the wisdom of good stewardship.

CHAPTER 10

INFORMATION IS POWER

Kate is twenty-two years old and has just started her first job after university. She is keen to get control of her finances before they take control of her. She has followed everything in this book so far and has prepared a budget that allows her to live a joyful and sacrificial life. She has thought about the changes in her life that her budget represents, and she is committed to seeing them through.

So she is surprised to see that this book has still more chapters! Isn't it enough to have a budget that is workable? Surely she doesn't need to do anything else? Or *does* she . . . ?

I used to work in the finance department of a clothing retailer. Every Monday morning my first job was to collect all the sales reports for the previous week and write a report for the head of sales and the finance director. It was important for them to be able to make decisions that affected the coming week, on the basis of the latest information.

In fact, whatever industry you work in, all the major decisions will require up-to-date information. Since the invention of the computer, the amount of information that any organization can gather, store and collate has increased massively. Conversely, the speed with which it is gathered and can be turned into a useful report has gone down.

In retail, for example, the computer system can be linked to the tills in all the stores, telling the company how much stock they currently hold. Stores might also have a footfall-counter under the welcome mat to determine how many people come in each day. Sales figures are updated instantly, so that someone in head office can see what is selling well and where, and make instant decisions about what stock should be moved to which parts of the country.

The more up to date the information, the more likely it is that the decisions will be the right ones. But if an organization does not hold up-to-date information, then, at best, decisions will be made on the basis of out-of-date data, and, at worst, on the basis of guesswork.

Information is the key

We have already seen this in practice. If you wrote down what you thought you spent every month and then kept records (see chapter 6), then you will have noticed that our guesswork is fallible, given that our hearts are deceptive and that we can persuade ourselves that something is true even when it is not, especially if it suits us to be so persuaded.

I often sit down with people to discuss their personal finances. When we get to this point, I very often find that they are quite excited. The process has given them an insight into their financial habits, and we have produced a plan that should help them live more wisely, just like Kate in our example.

Then I talk to them about record-keeping. Oh dear . . . It sounds so dull, so painful. Surely there are many better things to do with my time, more godly things? Frankly, most of us would rather watch paint dry.

There are two issues at stake here. First of all, we are interested in a *lifetime* of discipleship. This is not a once-and-for-all quick fix to a big problem. In six months', or six years' time, you cannot possibly make decisions based on information gathered today. That is especially true if you are successful in changing your habits in line with the budget now. The truth is that the information quickly becomes out of date.

Secondly, it is wishful thinking to assume that having a budget means that you will stick to it. It is all very well having a plan, but if you are not checking whether or not you are sticking to it, then how can you *know* that you are? We can even convince ourselves we *have* changed because we produced a budget, but *at the same time* keep living the way we were. It is easy to separate perception and reality when our hearts are deceitful.

> *To fail to plan is to plan to fail.*

Record-keeping sounds so mundane. And yet most organizations invest heavily in gathering and processing information because it is vital to the survival and growth of the enterprise. To fail to plan is to plan to fail. But to plan and then not monitor whether you are sticking to the plan is to waste your time planning in the first place.

The essence of godliness

Record-keeping may sound mundane, yet isn't it mundane things done for spiritual reasons that are the very essence of godly living? It's not that going to work or talking or being married (and the list goes endlessly on) are innately spiritual. But if they are done in a Christian way, and for gospel reasons, then they become the very things through which God furthers his purposes. It is what we say and do in the daily grind that really matters.

Frankly, I would rather not devote a chapter to record-keeping. It sounds boring. I even tried really hard to come up with a chapter title that sounded interesting, just to lure you in. I would love to have a line in the book somewhere that says, 'Just as you kept records for a month or two, now do it every month for ever.' Yet even at this stage in the book, there will be those who skipped the bit about keeping records for a month, and, if that was you, you are not very likely to keep them for ever unless I help you. And there will be others who were happy to do it for a couple of months but who baulk at the idea of doing it for ever. Our diaries are so full, and this does take time.

Yet if you *are* one of the people who didn't keep records for a month or two earlier on, then you will know exactly how hard it is to prepare a budget without that information, information which is the key to wise and accurate decision-making.

So I want to commend record-keeping to you. Let's see why it is so important and then think about how to do it in a way that doesn't take up too much time.

Most excellent!

Earlier we went to Corinth to see Paul encourage the believers to be like the Macedonians. At the end of that section of 2 Corinthians 8, Paul says:

> **But as you excel in everything – in faith, in speech, in knowledge, in all earnestness, and in our love for you – see that you excel in this act of grace also.**
> (2 Corinthians 8:7)

The act of grace is the collection for the saints. Paul puts it in a category with a number of other spiritual disciplines, none of which we find naturally easy. The worldly, fleshly self has suppressed the truth about God (Romans 1:18), so knowledge of God and his gospel, and in particular faith in that God and gospel, are not common in our sinful nature. Consequently, neither is godly speech, earnestness in godly living, or love within the covenant community. They are all of grace, all brought about by the power of the gospel in us. Paul could have listed any number of other things: perhaps prayer and the service of the church. But the point is clear: just as the converted person must be disciplined, trained in godliness in each area, so he must be trained in godliness with money. It will not happen without effort. But this is something we will grow in, just as we grow in knowledge and other areas.

Paul encourages the discipline of making and sticking to plans.

Rapid response

Not only does discipline in this area help us to monitor our success in sticking to the budget we have made, but when our plans need to change we have current information on which to base the new plans.

I can think of half a dozen life events (such as changing jobs and parenthood) that have meant considerable changes to our family circumstances. Some have required quick decisions that themselves required up-to-date information. You can't always see such situations coming. So you will need up-to-date records *all the time* in order to respond in a timely manner.

A new debtors' prison

The threat of debtors' prison and of having to sell oneself into slavery to pay debts, as was frequently the case around the time the Bible was written, meant that financial nous was essential to the survival of the family and the family business.

With the free availability of credit today, we have on the whole not needed to be disciplined with money in order to survive. I am of the opinion, however, that we do need to be disciplined if we are to avoid a new kind of imprisonment, to debt and bad financial practice. We need to go back to the habits that were common in previous generations. Besides, life is more complicated now, so we need to be even more on the ball.

If we want to use all that belongs to God for his glory, rather than our own, then we need to be willing to take practical steps to ensure that we have the right information with which to make decisions. If the heart is deceitful, then we need an objective source of information.

Numbers are information
We saw earlier that numbers generally often carry information.

The context of the numbers
Numbers that represent money also carry information. For example, we each know what £100 is worth to us. Let me prove that to you. What is your immediate reaction to the following two statements?

- Last month I spent £100 on food.
- Last month I spent £100 on coffee.

In each case the number is the same. Yet what that number represents is very different. Intuitively, we think that £100 for food is not a lot of money. And because we know that food is necessary to sustain life, we probably think that I did quite well to get all the food I needed to live on for £100.

On the other hand, coffee is more of a luxury. I could do

without it and still be alive. So to spend £100 a month on it seems quite a lot.

The same number, then (once we understand what it represents in each context), allows us to form opinions about how we are living and make decisions to change. Furthermore, because everyone knows *why* they make the decisions that they do (for example, I might spend a lot of time in coffee shops meeting with friends to study the Bible), they already understand the context of their own numbers.

Responding to the numbers
Indeed, in the case of the coffee example above, keeping accurate records allows me to make the decision to halve my coffee intake, thus saving £600 per year. My ongoing record-keeping allows me to assess whether or not I am sticking to my plan. Without ongoing records, the only certain way for me to reduce my coffee intake is to stop going to coffee shops altogether.

That sort of analysis is especially true of areas where our spending on any given occasion can be totally elastic. I am likely to spend roughly the same amount in a coffee shop each time I go. But what about going out for dinner? I could spend £10 one night and £100 the next. That means it wouldn't be enough to decide to cut the *frequency* of meals out, without limiting the *amount* I could spend on any given visit.

Since we know the context of those numbers, we can understand the information they represent instinctively. We just need the numbers.

Where the rubber hits the road
I hope that you are now persuaded, if you weren't already, that we need to keep good records. You should, I hope, at this stage be asking, 'How?'

The answer may be different for each one of us. The Bible tells us to be godly with money but doesn't prescribe how. I suggest that we begin with the advice below, and you can tweak or totally change it to fit your circumstances and personality.

The aim here, remember, is to preserve enough information to be useful, but not so much detail that the process becomes cumbersome, leading us to give up.

How complicated is your life?
There are at least three options for keeping financial records. You could keep them in a book (and you can buy ledger books for this very purpose from many stationery shops). But if you are more technically savvy, you could keep them on a spreadsheet. Alternatively, you could opt for a computer program that keeps records for you. The deciding factor here is how complicated your financial situation is at the moment and how easy you find each option.

If your financial circumstances are quite simple, with only one bank account, for example, then you might opt to keep records in a ledger book. This is relatively slow because you have to add the columns yourself (which increases the risk of error), but it is user-friendly for a less computer-literate generation.

The more complicated your life, the more you will need to think about computerizing the process. Most of us will find life becoming more complex as we get older and have to deal with mortgages, credit cards and the like. So it is worth considering moving to a computerized system as soon as possible.

A spreadsheet is really just a computerized ledger, but it has the advantage of being as big as you want (for multiple bank accounts) and doing the sums for you (thus removing some errors).

However, unless you get along well with spreadsheets, you may find that you want something more user-friendly still.

There is a range of downloadable programs on the internet that will allow you to keep detailed records simply, and enable you to look at the information by category, payee or account, or in total. This flexibility is really useful when making decisions. Much of the data is usually exportable into spreadsheets, so that you can manipulate it as you need to.

You may need to seek help, to begin with, to run such a program, if you do not use computers much, but it is very simple to use and saves a lot of time, once you know your way around.

How much detail do you really want?
The next issue is how much detail you really want. The level is totally up to you: you may think it sufficient to have a dozen broad categories, or you might want the detail in 100 categories. In practice, at least if you use a spreadsheet or other computer program, increasing the level of detail doesn't especially increase the workload, but it does give you a better handle on what is going on.

There are, however, limits. In theory, you could have a list that is 1,000 items long and details every type of magazine you buy and every shop you visit. Clearly this is excessive, and the volume of information obscures its usefulness. In the main, therefore, I recommend that you make a decision about the level of detail based on an arbitrary standard. I tend to think that if we spend more than £100 per year on any given item, then it deserves its own category.

For example, when I first did this, I kept all food items together. As I have admitted, though, I was spending too much on food, so I split this further into 'groceries' and 'going out' (and we have subsequently added 'entertaining', for what we buy to cook for others). This allowed me to see what I was really spending on necessary food and what was discretionary and needed set limits.

You may find that the same sort of division is needed for bigger items, but also that you can draw several smaller categories into one.

Always the aim is to choose a level that gives you as much control as you need. If you find that you lack sufficient information about one category, then you probably ought to split it further. This is a tool where the purpose is to help you to be godly now and in the future, so get used to making changes in how you analyse things as soon as the need becomes apparent. Over time, your system will evolve into something that maps your life accurately without being unduly cumbersome.

Three useful tips
Here are three tips that I have found helpful.

First, you may find that you need extra detail for those areas where you know you struggle to be self-controlled. The very act of splitting that category into quite small areas allows you to keep yourself better informed.

Secondly, have a catch-all category for all those items that are too small to warrant a category of their own, too unusual to fit into a regular category, or totally unexpected and unplanned.

I call this our 'miscellaneous' category, and pretty much anything can go into it, so it can vary quite a lot from month to month. For example, a couple of years ago we had to get our drain unblocked, and it cost £120. We didn't have anything in the budget for that because it was totally unexpected, so it went into 'miscellaneous'. Some months you will go over budget and some months under. That is natural and cannot be predicted with any certainty.

Over time you might find that some items come up regularly enough for you to put a line in the budget for them in future years. Typically, if 'miscellaneous' is high, then it means that you don't have enough categories.

Finally, you need to cut the *right* corners in order to save time. For example, my family don't collect receipts for *everything* we spend. Often you won't be offered a receipt at your corner shop, for example. Make a point of noting down all that *isn't* food, and you'll find that the difference between the cash you have taken out and the contents of your purse or wallet is what you have spent on food.

How often should we update records?
How regularly you update records is up to you entirely, but let me give you a couple of cautions. The more often you do it, the easier it is to find the time. If you update your records every day, then it will take only a couple of minutes, so you can do it while supper is cooking, for example. The day is fresh in your memory, and you will know exactly what you have spent.

On the other hand, if you intend to do it monthly you need to realize that you will have to carve out an hour (probably more initially). There are two further drawbacks. First, the longer you leave it, the more time you will need. If you find it hard to carve out an hour this month, leaving it until the following month means that you will need to find at least two hours then.

Secondly, the quality of the information that you can capture goes down over time, because you forget what you spent, where and why. Even with receipts, it is often difficult to remember what you spent the money on and for what purpose.

I therefore suggest that you aim to update records approximately weekly, though each person's life is different, and you will need to find the timescale that suits you.

What do we want to see?
Later on we will look at how we might use the monthly information to help us anticipate the future and protect ourselves

against our own bad habits. For the time being, however, let me give a couple of tips on what we want to see and how to get there.

You will find that the most useful information ends up in the same basic format as your budget. So, if your budget looks something like the one in chapter 8, then it is good to get your actual records to follow the same pattern.

Most of the downloadable programs will produce such a report, but just a few words to those who will use another method.

If you use a spreadsheet or ledger book, then your monthly record might look like this:

January	Fixed necessary exp.			Fixed necessary exp.			Long-term financial plan			Total
	Rent	Council tax	Electricity	Food	Travel	Phones	Savings	Family	Etc.	
1st	1,000						300	250		2,000
2nd				50	25					100
3rd										0
4th		75	70							145
Etc.										
Total	1,000	75	70	220	70	40	300	250		2,500

At the end of the month, I suggest that you take the totals from the bottom and put them into a summary schedule in a similar format to your budget. This will make comparing the two much easier and allow you to take a step back from the fine detail to see what has happened overall in the month and the year.

Conclusion
In the next chapter we will look at how to make the best use of the gathered information. I hope that you are now beginning

to see the benefits of keeping records. It is a relatively easy discipline to learn, and it becomes natural over time, but it does require determination to begin with. With this information at your fingertips, you can now make decisions based on fact, not on fiction.

Study questions:

1. In our opening scenario, how would you advise Kate? How are you different from her and how would you advise yourself?
2. What will be the best method for you to use to keep records?
3. How will you make time to keep records properly, without allowing this to conflict with other important aspects of your life?

CHAPTER 11

'EXCEL IN THIS ACT OF GRACE ALSO'

> Christina is pleased with herself. She has prepared a budget and worked out how she will stick to it. She has kept records for the past three months and seems to be managing OK.
>
> However, she can also see some changes on the horizon that will affect her current budget. She may need to change jobs in the next few weeks, but she doesn't know what that will mean for her budget. Will it really be completely out of date so soon after she has prepared it?

We've seen how recording information helps us to reach our spiritual target of honouring God with our money. But what can we do with that information, and, in particular, how we can adapt to changing circumstances?

Let's look at the review process. This is where we see the real benefit of setting targets (budgeting) and then keeping records.

Keep your finger on the pulse

Let us take Christina's situation. What she really needs is an updated budget, containing the budget going forward, *as well as* the past couple of months' actual figures. This is called a forecast.

A forecast is simply a copy of the budget, say from January to December, on to which we put the real figures for each past month. This allows us to see, side by side, the real financial history to date and the plans for the future that we started out with. We then have a budget that is up to date and which we can tweak in order to see the effect of our changed circumstances.

Remember that we are concerned most of all with ensuring that Christina doesn't run out of cash. The forecast allows us to check that at any time. As soon as we become aware of changes in circumstances, then we can reflect them in the forecast. When we set the budget, we needed to be prudent about forecasting changes, erring on the side of caution. We can alter the forecast as those circumstantial changes become reality.

Let's look more closely at Christina's situation, using the following forecast. January to March are actual figures, April to September budgeted figures.

	Jan	Feb	Mar	Apr	May	Jun	Jul	Aug	Sep	Total
Income	1,500	1,500	1,500	1,500	1,500	1,500	1,500	1,500	1,500	**13,500**
Food	200	210	180	150	150	150	150	150	150	1,490
Phone	60	60	60	50	50	50	50	50	50	480
Travel	90	80	90	100	100	100	100	100	100	860
Other exp.	900	900	900	900	900	900	900	900	900	8,100
Holidays				500				500		1,000
One-off items		500			600				500	1,600
Total exp.	1,250	1,750	1,230	1,700	1,800	1,200	1,200	1,700	1,700	**13,530**
Movement	250	(250)	270	(200)	(300)	300	300	(200)	(200)	**(30)**
Balance	250	–	270	70	(230)	70	370	170	(30)	**(30)**

Changes worth considering

As we look at this illustration, there are three types of change worth considering.

First, our **assumptions** may be wrong. So, in Christina's case, her assumption about how much she would spend on food was incorrect. This will happen in many areas at the beginning, because Christina prepared the budget on the basis of only one or two months' information. She may have tried to cut too much off her shopping bill and she will need to adjust her forecast for the rest of the year in order to reflect the reality as it is now seen.

Secondly, the assumptions may have been right at the time, but her **circumstances** are changing and the assumptions are no longer valid. This is not uncommon. Consider Christina's income. She was able to be completely accurate with that, but, with the new job situation, the figure is likely to change. She will need to make a reasonable, though conservative, adjustment to her income figures.

Thirdly, every so often we will want to ask, '**How have I changed?**' This will not always be immediately obvious, but the gospel will change every Christian over time. Our loves and hates, interests and commitments alter as the word of Christ dwells in us richly. So it shouldn't be a surprise, for example, when giving that felt sacrificial last year might not feel very sacrificial any more. In this context, it is worth asking: 'What might I change today to reflect how I have changed?'

Being aware of these three considerations will help every time we review, and, in particular, plan the next year's budget.

Remember that our overall aim is to help us to honour God with every penny that enters our control. This process of plan–record–review allows us to exercise proper control at any given point.

What might Christina do?

Let us go back to Christina's scenario.

The first thing to realize is that she will run out of money in May and September. This is really important because it tells us that something needs to change.

Secondly, we need to see that she has underestimated her outgoings. She will have to think about whether or not she can spend only £150 per month on food, as, at present, she is over budget by almost £50 per month. Does March tell us that she is getting her food costs under control or not? Only Christina will know. The same questions apply to phone and travel costs. Are the causes of the variations ongoing, or did she have friends staying with her who ate a lot and spent every evening on the phone?

Let us assume that the trends we can see will continue. What can Christina do?

She can solve the problem in May by not paying for her summer holiday in April. By moving that payment until she has enough money (to June for example), Christina can avoid being overdrawn in May.

I would encourage her not to include upward adjustments to her income until either she has a new job (with contract signed) or her employer tells her that she will receive a pay rise. It would be easy to assume that she can sort out the deficit with an imaginary pay rise, but that will leave her worse off, if it fails to materialize.

And we still have the problem of September. Christina will want to look through her outgoings and see where she could tighten her belt. Perhaps she *can* make radical changes to her food-buying after all. Perhaps a change of mobile-phone supplier or mode of transport would solve the problem. In general, if caught early enough, a combination of small changes will solve quite big problems.

However, even if such changes are not possible, there are other solutions. The obvious one would be to have a cheaper holiday, or no holiday at all. By reducing the holiday cost to £600, Christina can easily live within her means without changing anything else. Holidays are often entirely discretionary

– we may not need to go away on holiday, even if we *feel* that we do, and it is often possible to save very large amounts in this area of discretionary spending.

All Christina needs to do now is adjust the forecast to reflect the changes she is making, and then stick to it.

Easy when you know how

This process may seem alien at first, but the principles are easy to grasp, and I don't think it takes very long to think through the process for yourself. The advantage is that you know yourself and, almost instinctively, you will know whether your assumptions are wrong or whether you are just not being disciplined enough.

Reviewing like this doesn't need to take very long, and has the advantage that, done often enough, you can predict problems so far in advance that you will make the necessary adjustments without losing sleep.

It really does pay to keep reviewing regularly.

And here we go again

Towards the end of the year we will need to start again, preparing the budget for the next year. Each year, as the amount of information we have gathered increases, the better we become at preparing a budget that fits our life. Even when we are predicting big changes, like the arrival of children, the process allows us to enter the future, confident about our finances.

Start with the forecast from the present year, which is now nearly full of actual figures, as the basis for next year's budget. Extend that forward for another year, paying careful attention to annual trends, remembering that the next budget follows on from the present forecast. We will then need to adjust for any one-off events in the year just gone by that probably won't be repeated in the following year.

Finally, so far as you can, factor in the changes in circumstances that you can predict.

In total, I think this process should take about an hour, though I appreciate that the more uncertainty there is about the future, the more time you will need.

What's at stake

What might this do to the church? How might this change us all for the better? (Those are the questions that we'll look at in the final chapter.) Are you willing to be changed? If you have read this far, then I trust that you are. Matthew 6:24 reminds us what is at stake:

> **No one can serve two masters, for either he will hate the one and love the other, or he will be devoted to the one and despise the other. You cannot serve God and money.**

You can let money lead your heart away from God, or you can put God first and control the money. What you can't do, according to Jesus, is be devoted to God and money at the same time.

Of this passage, Craig Blomberg says: 'It is arguable that materialism is the single biggest competitor with authentic Christianity for the hearts and souls of millions in our world today, including many in the visible church.'[1]

CHAPTER 12

GIVE AS GOOD AS YOU GET

Our current UK tax system benefits the giver. We will use a higher-rate taxpayer to make this point because it allows us to see just how beneficial giving can be. However, I hope that this will also act as a useful guide for all of us. The principle, as we will see, is that the system benefits the generous.

> Tim is a doctor in Leeds. He has become persuaded that God needs to direct his use of money. Tim earns £100,000 per year and has calculated that his family need £20,000. Tim is concerned to use as much of that money for gospel causes as possible, but he pays more than £40,000 per year in tax and national insurance. How can Tim organize his finances in order to maximize the gospel use of that money?

Tax incentives for charitable giving
The government allows charities and churches to claim back tax on gifts made by UK taxpayers. It does this because those charities provide a service that meets a need in society which the government cannot provide for. The UK government treats such gifts as though they were made before tax is applied.[1]

Provided the donor has paid sufficient tax in the given tax year (up to 5 April in the UK), then the government will refund to the charity 25p for every £1 given, and each £1 you give to charity by Gift Aid reduces the tax you pay by 25 pence, right up to the point where you pay no tax at all.

That means that if Tim gave the balancing (almost) £40,000 to church and charities, then they could claim an additional (nearly) £10,000 from the government, thus reducing his tax payments and increasing the amount available for gospel causes.

The higher-rate taxpayer

And there is an additional incentive for the higher-rate taxpayer. Every penny earned over the first £43,875 (in 2010/11) is taxed at 40%. The Gift Aid scheme assumes that gifts were originally taxed at 20%, and so the charity claims 25% (20/80) in gift aid. The difference is reclaimable by the *donor* through their self-assessment tax return.

Let's consider Tim's last £10,000 of income. He has had £4,000 of tax taken off. Now let's suppose that Tim gives the remaining £6,000 to his church. The government gives back the standard rate tax: £1,500 (20/80 × £6,000), which increases the total to £7,500. The government retains the balancing £2,500 of the original earnings of £10,000.

Through his tax return, Tim can reclaim that £2,500. Although this will arrive a long time after the original gift is made, it reduces the effective cost of the gift from £6,000 to just £3,500. The church gets £7,500 because Tim gave them £3,500![2]

The incentive for higher-rate taxpayers to give substantially is, in consequence, very high. For Tim to give all of his excess would greatly benefit the church, at a lower cost to himself, as it is the taxman whose income is most affected.

If Tim were to repeat this exercise in the second year, he would be able to live on £20,000 of the total rebate from the government and give even more of his taxed income away. By doing this, Tim can reduce his tax payments to less than 6% of his income and his gifts to church to nearly £60,000 a year! We might represent this as follows:

	Year 1	Y/e adjust	Year 2	Y/e adjust	Year 2	Y/e adjust
Income	£100,000		£100,000		£100,000	
Tax (roughly)	(£29,900)		(£29,900)		(£29,900)	
NI (roughly)	(£4,700)		(£4,700)		(£4,700)	
Net income	£65,400		£65,400		£65,400	
Rebate (roughly)	–	£14,170	£14,170	£14,170	£14,170	
Giving	(£45,400)		£59,570		£59,570	
Left to live on	£20,000		£20,000		£20,000	
Total to HMRC	£34,600	(£25,520)	£34,600	(£29,060)	£34,600	(£29,060)
Total to church	£45,400	£11,350	£59,570	£14,890	£59,570	£14,890
Total due to self	£20,000	£14,170	£20,000	£14,170	£20,000	£14,170

In any year, after the first, the total income of the donor will be their earned income *plus* the rebate due from HM Revenue and Customs for any higher-rate gifts in the previous year. Thus the tax-free income covers the cost of living, and the entire taxable income can be given away!

A questionable practice?

But is this an ethical practice? Under normal circumstances we ought to pay X tax, so should we pay much less than this? Yes. The government has organized the tax system so that this is an entirely legitimate practice that supports organizations that the government deems to be important. The question is rather whether it is ethical *not* to make use of the tax system in order to maximize the benefit to the church. We are told to give to the government the tax that is owed, but our responsibility to steward God's resources demands that we be careful not to give more.

Clearly this scenario will not match most people's situation. Either your income or your necessary outgoings, and probably both, will not match Tim's circumstances. Nevertheless, this fairly extreme situation does challenge us to live wholeheartedly for God and begins to show us the sort of tax-efficient decisions that we might make.

★   ★   ★

We are not, like the rich man in Mark 10, being commanded to give up all our possessions in order to be fit to follow Jesus. But if we are *unwilling* to give them all up, then we haven't even begun to grasp the warning of Matthew 6.

Perhaps Craig Blomberg is right to call his book *Neither Poverty nor Riches*. We need to have the wisdom of the writer of Proverbs today, which could serve as a 'model prayer':

> **Two things I ask of you;**
> **deny them not to me before I die:**
> **Remove far from me falsehood and lying;**
> **give me neither poverty nor riches;**
> **feed me with the food that is needful for me,**
> **lest I be full and deny you**
> **and say, 'Who is the LORD?'**
> **or lest I be poor and steal**
> **and profane the name of my God.**
> (Proverbs 30:7–9)

Study questions:

1. What are your probable changes in circumstances over the next year, and how are they likely to affect your financial planning?
2. How often will you review your records in order to ensure that you are sticking to your budget?
3. Will you pray the Proverbs prayer? Whom can you ask to help you to be faithful to it?

CHAPTER 13

MAKING THE MOST OF YOUR DEATH

It doesn't take a genius to work out that one out of every one person dies (Enoch and Elijah didn't die, but Lazarus and the son of the widow died twice, so it balances out!). One hundred per cent. We can't avoid death, and we can't really predict when it will happen until it gets very close. Yet we can make decisions about what we would like to happen to our estate when we die.

Phil has just turned sixty and, with the recent birth of his first grandchild, he is thinking about how he can best use the wealth that he has accumulated. During his personal devotions, he came across this verse:

A good man leaves an inheritance to his children's children,
but the sinner's wealth is laid up for the righteous.
(Proverbs 13:22)

Phil has come to you for advice: does this mean that the most godly thing to do is leave as much wealth as possible to his grandchildren?

What is an inheritance?
The above might sound like a silly question, but I think it is a profound one. In the Bible, an inheritance is a share in God's promises. We find that idea in Proverbs:

> **Whoever misleads the upright into an evil way**
> **will fall into his own pit,**
> **but the blameless will have a goodly inheritance.**
> (Proverbs 28:10)

The inheritance began as a share in the promised land of Canaan (e.g. Psalm 105:11). Every Jubilee year the land was to be returned to the family who originally owned it, so that every family retained their inheritance. The people, in turn, were to be God's inheritance (e.g. Psalm 78:71).

This trajectory continues into the New Testament. First, we are told that Israel (the pleasant vineyard, the land) belongs to the son as an inheritance (e.g. Mark 12:7). The inheritance is clearly the new creation – all the nations that have become the possession of their one king, Jesus. God still has the saints as his inheritance (Ephesians 1:18), and the church in turn inherits his kingdom with Jesus (1 Peter 1:4; cf. Ephesians 1:11, 14; Colossians 1:12, 3:24; Hebrews 9:15).

In other words, the inheritance that we should really want is that which comes by faith to those who trust in Jesus. Our inheritance is imperishable, waiting for us where Jesus is, and it's *not* whatever we do or do not have in this life. By extension, the inheritance that we must strive to pass on to our children's children will be the gospel, through which they too can obtain an inheritance worth having. And our aspiration must be that we pass on with it models of gospel living that will keep our family in good stead spiritually after we have gone.

Obviously we will want to look after our children and grand-children in other ways too. But, as we remember God's priorities for his money, we may choose *not* to leave wealth to those who will use it inappropriately. Our aim is to benefit our children spiritually first, and then, when they know how to use that wealth for the glory of God, to benefit them materially.

Remember Bible principle 2: 'Everything belongs to God.' Everything we might acquire in life, everything we might pass on, is God's. Our responsibility is always to do what most honours him. If we have raised our children to understand that all money belongs to him, then they will also understand that any inheritance we leave is not exempt. So our first con-sideration, in either giving or receiving an inheritance, is to ask what will most bring glory to God.

Naked we come into the world . . .

Obviously, Phil is looking ahead to his own death, so we will begin with his family. Our first question is: *for whom does he have responsibility?* The closer the family ties and the fewer the other responsible family members, the more responsible he is for those relatives. It would be good for Phil to make a list, acknowledging that this may lead to caring for cousins in need ahead of his own children who may not be in need.

The next question would be: *do **they** act responsibly?* If Phil were to leave them money, would they know how to use it wisely? If Phil has a relative in need, but that need is created by a gambling habit, for example, leaving wealth to that person would be like pouring oil on a fire. It would be totally irrespon-sible. Consider what happened to the prodigal son who inherited great wealth. He certainly ended up worse off than if he had not received it. Is there evidence of wisdom in general and, as importantly, Christian wisdom? It is much wiser to leave wealth to someone who shows every sign of being governed by God's priorities, because that wealth will do that person much less damage if they are wise.

I would therefore caution us against the tendency to leave everything to unbelieving children who will then squander what belongs to God. He has given us his money, and we should always aim to give it back to him – and no time could be more appropriate than when we are preparing to meet him!

Clearly we need to be very careful here, for there is a danger of creating great bitterness by showing favouritism. We need to be seen to be scrupulously fair, open and honest about our motivations. The worst thing we could do for the gospel is to die, leaving our families with wrong expectations about our intentions and no means of understanding why we made our decisions. But if we are making decisions that are consistent with the way we have lived our lives, and if we have explained those decisions, then our children will understand our motivations.

> *God has given us his money, and we should always aim to give it back to him – and no time could be more appropriate than when we are preparing to meet him!*

The third question we might ask is: *where are the real needs?* Parents of young children need to consider very carefully how they would be looked after in the event of their death. Phil isn't in this situation, but many of us will be. It may be appropriate, for a time, to take out life insurance to mitigate the financial hardships our loved ones would face. Over time, and as those children become independent, so the needs change, and the will that we prepare needs to be altered too. It is wise every couple of years, as our family circumstances change, to stop and ask where the real needs lie.

The fourth question is: *to what extent is it wiser to give to gospel causes directly?* I suspect that a lot of Christians leave money to their children, assuming that it will be used wisely. But we can't assume anything. Instead, why not talk through the options with your children now? Not only does it prevent recriminations and confusion when the will is read, but it helps the family to decide what to do with God's money. It also gives you a useful insight into how spiritually mature your children really are!

The final question to ask is: *when?* In general, I suggest that we plan to provide for our own needs until death and give everything else away while we are still alive. Obviously, we want to avoid being a burden to others, so it is right to have a home and an income through retirement.

However, we can still choose how big our home is and where, how much we have in savings, and so on. It is wise to 'give away as we go', for two reasons. First, because we get to control where the money goes, and, secondly, because the smaller our estate is, the less we will have to pay in death duties (such as inheritance tax in the UK). And the lower the tax, the better use we can make of the wealth God has entrusted to us.

A friend of mine recently told me that his eighty-four-year-old father lives alone in a large house, and that the inheritance tax on his estate will exceed £300,000. How much wiser it would be to sell the house now and give all that is not needed to worthy recipients. Over time, this practice becomes untaxable.[1]

Whose wealth is it anyway?
A total of 70% of the UK population owned their own home in 2003 / 4, up 25% from 1981.[2] A large proportion of the population will leave property to others in their wills. Many of us, therefore, will receive a bit of an inheritance somewhere along the way. A good question to ask, when receiving it, is: what will most benefit the gospel?

In Proverbs 30:7–9 the writer prays against poverty so that he doesn't become poor and sink to stealing, thus bringing God's name into disrepute. At the same time, he prays against riches, lest he should forget his dependence on God and deny him.

When we think about how to use an inheritance, the same prayer might be a good model. The inheritance might be a gift from God to deal with our own potential poverty, or it might be a gift that we can give away in order to bless others. In the latter case, it would be unwise to let it burn a hole in our pockets.

So which course of action will help the kingdom of God to grow in the world and in me? How might the course of action I choose help me to grow to be more like Jesus? Can I loosen my grip on this world to tighten my grip on the next? How can I make the most of my death?

CHAPTER 14

RADICAL CHURCH

We've seen examples (some real, some not), but the test is whether or not all that we have said effects a change in you, the reader. How has this book challenged you so far?

Indeed, if it has challenged you, how might it challenge the wider culture in your church? What have you read that your pastor needs to hear, or that your house group could put into practice, or that your children could benefit from? The rest is up to you.

What we have said so far may seem pretty mundane. But in many ways, as we've seen, living the Christian life is really about doing the everyday things for God and not for the gods of our age. Now I want to take a step back and ask us to imagine what it might look like if the whole church were to be radical with money.

Where we're at
In the first chapter we considered the default culture. We know we ought to be different, yet so often we talk the talk much better than we walk the walk. Of our attitude to giving,

for example, Alcorn speaks of our miserly attitudes when he says:

> **Too often we imagine we are asking God's Spirit for guidance, when actually we are relying on our culture-driven values. No wonder our decisions end up looking suspiciously like everyone else's.**[1]

When we are indistinguishable from the culture around us, then there is something badly wrong. The problem is that we live in a culture where 'we major in the momentary and minor in the momentous'.[2]

This takes us back to Bible principle 4: the heart is deceitful above all things, so don't trust it. We can easily convince ourselves that we are being godly, yet we don't like to talk about how we are doing in case people know what we are *really* like. Of course there is a place for appropriate modesty, but Jesus would warn us to check whether or not we are even admitting our deceit to ourselves:

> **For everyone who does wicked things hates the light and does not come to the light, lest his works should be exposed. But whoever does what is true comes to the light, so that it may be clearly seen that his works have been carried out in God.** (John 3:20–21)

As churches, we need to be prepared to talk openly about money and how we idolize it, how we misuse it, and what we might do about that. Alcorn says, 'We should be careful to surround ourselves with biblically based advisors, who do not resist but embrace the promptings of God's Spirit to give.'[3] We desperately need wisdom, and the church needs to identify people with the appropriate wisdom so that we can grow up together in this area.

Changed beliefs and changed lives

At the heart of all the advice, we need the word of God. Without this, we will fail to motivate one another to lasting change.

We noted Bible principle 5: real change flows from a firm grasp of the gospel, by the Spirit. This refers to the church as well as to the individual. That is why churches that mature people into joyful servants of Christ are the ones that bring the whole counsel of God to the congregation. As we 'gospel one another', we bring change in the heart that, in turn, changes lives.

It would be easy to become Pharisees here, and for change to be motivated by guilt or by the promise of spiritual rewards. And it is true that God rewards us lavishly for doing well with what he gives us. But all change in the Christian life should stem from a grasp of what *God* has done for *us*, not the other way round.

Up the ante

But, of course, that sort of change is dangerous. A church that grasps the gospel and is willing to be radical will be a church that stands out. People asking 'What can I give?' rather than 'What can I get?' will make decisions on a completely different basis from that of the world.

It might, for example, be a church whose members reduce their working hours to become more involved in the work of the fellowship or to spend time with their families. It will certainly contain people who remain in their jobs, but who, as they climb the career ladder, will look increasingly different from their peers. As your salary increases, and the amount you give away increases too, so the difference in lifestyle between you and your peers will grow. Noticeably so.

Remember Bible principle 3: be like your heavenly Father: generous? This is exemplified for me in the story of John Wesley, which you can find almost everywhere in literature on the subject of giving. His phrase 'Gain all you can, save all you can, give all you can'[4] is exemplified by his own life.

> In 1731 Wesley began to limit his expenses so he would have more money to give to the poor. He records that one year his income was £30, and his living expenses £28, so he had £2 to give away. The next year, his income doubled, but he still lived on £28 and gave £32 away. In the third year, his income jumped to £90; again he lived on £28, giving away £62. The fourth year, he made £120, lived on £28 and gave £92 to the poor.
>
> Wesley preached that Christians should not merely tithe, but give away all extra income once the family and creditors were taken care of. He believed that, with increasing income, the Christian's standard of *giving* should increase, not his standard of living . . . One year his income was slightly over £1,400; he gave away all but £30.[5]

Wesley preached that Christians should not merely tithe, but give away all extra income once the family and creditors were taken care of.

Now imagine a whole congregation living like that, imagine the whole church in the West living like that. The fact that it is so hard to imagine tells us just how far from that scenario we are at the moment. Cicero said that 'gratitude is the mother of all virtues'. He was right. Our thanks to God will drive us to gracious living.

Whose cares win?

Not only are we to be generous, as our Father is, but we are to be generous *for the things he cares about*. Bible principle 2 was: God owns everything. This needs to shape our attitudes. In particular, we need to have God's attitude to one another in the church. We are all part of the one body, the new man in Christ (Ephesians 2:15). We must care for all the spiritual and physical needs of the church. Has God given the church all that it needs to care for its own? God promises to give what we need. Perhaps, then, the reason that there are so many needy Christians in the world is because he has given to the church as a whole, and those of us with much haven't passed it on.

It is tempting to think that, if there are no obvious needs in my congregation, I can use the money as I like. But all of the church should recognize its interdependence, at the local and global level. We should be honest, about both our needs and our ability to meet those needs. The local church needs to model this, as those who require help come forward and receive from those with much. This needn't be just financial. There are many ways that this could work if we were creative.

For example, there is a radical church in Seattle that raises funds so that young first-time home buyers can pay cash for property, rather than acquire a mortgage. This has many benefits: they avoid even this debt; they model their interdependence on one another in church; and they free up all the money that would have been spent on interest payments, for the sake of the gospel.[6]

Others might consider giving generously *through* the local church. If we find ourselves with excess this month and do not have immediate needs to meet, we could give to the church, allowing the church to administer aid in an Acts 6 way to our own congregation. But it also allows the church to support mission, theological colleges, church plants or churches in the suffering two-thirds world.

Done as a church, this has the advantage that each recipient can be properly assessed by the church as a whole to ensure that they are suitable to be helped, given the priorities that God has for his church.

There are plenty of other things that, as congregations, we own and could share: power tools, books, cars and property, for example. How many copies of a given book does your congregation need? How many spare bedrooms? All of them could be put at the disposal of the whole church and, in total, save the church a lot of money. It is more fashionable to own than to borrow, but it isn't more godly. Especially when you consider that it all belongs to God and should be held in common by the church.

The radical church

So what change could you make? What difference could your church make if we grasped this vision? An other-person-centred church being radical with its possessions could shine out in a society that loves darkness. If we would step out of that darkness, put our lamp on its stand, be the city on the hill, shining in the darkness, how attractive the gospel would be (John 13:35).

But if it were possible to be what our highest aspirations would have us be, then God wouldn't need to prepare the new creation for us. We are not yet the perfected humanity that we will one day be. We will still be selfish, and ungrateful at times. And it will require time and the gospel to change us even into what we *can* be. But by grace we can get there. Shortly before his death in 1807, John Newton said:

> **I am not what I ought to be. I am not what I want to be. I am not what I hope to be. But still, I am not what I used to be. And by the grace of God, I am what I am.**[7]

In the end

Remember where we are going. Revelation 7:9–10 describes the one church as 'a great multitude that no one could number, from every nation, from all tribes and peoples and languages, standing before the throne and before the Lamb, clothed in white robes, with palm branches in their hands, and crying out with a loud voice, "Salvation belongs to our God who sits on the throne, and to the Lamb!"'

The church will worship Jesus, the Lamb who was slain, with one voice. Differences that spoil our communion now will be healed, and all tears wiped away by the hand of God himself. I love this verse because it speaks of the reason for the transformation that will happen to all of us:

Beloved, we are God's children now, and what we will be has not yet appeared; but we know that when he appears we shall be like him, because we shall see him as he is. (1 John 3:2)

One day we will see Jesus as he is and then we will be like him. The perfect knowledge of the perfect Son will transform the church into the perfect image of that Son for all eternity.

In the words of Randy Alcorn, 'May what will be most important to us five minutes after we die become most important to us now.'[8]

Ten commitments to change

The following ten commitments are an attempt to summarize the challenge of the Bible's teaching on money. If you have been persuaded of the case I have made, why not join me in making these commitments as a response to all that you have seen?

- I commit to live my life now, in view of the end, looking forward to the new creation.
- I commit to turn everything I am and have over to God, the rightful owner.
- I commit to a generous lifestyle, considering how generous my heavenly Father has been to me.
- I commit to acknowledging my sinful heart and seeking the wisdom of others in important decisions.
- I commit to asking God, by his Spirit, to change me through the gospel.
- I commit to a lifestyle that differs from that of the world around me.
- I commit to making plans governed by God's priorities for me, my family, his church and the world.
- I commit to reviewing how well I am keeping to those plans, knowing that my heart will deceive me.
- I commit to seeking the spiritual growth of my church in the area of money.
- I commit to being a radical disciple of Jesus Christ.

BIBLIOGRAPHY AND USEFUL RESOURCES

Randy Alcorn – *Money, Possessions and Eternity* (Wheaton, IL: Tyndale House Publishers, 2003 edition)
I had to import this book from the USA (a shame that it isn't more widely available). It covers just about every subject that you could think of, which makes it 500 pages long. It is a useful reference, with many insightful practical comments. It needs to be read in the light of the Bible's wider context.

Craig L. Blomberg – *Neither Poverty Nor Riches* (Nottingham: IVP: Apollos, 2003 edition)
A biblical theology of money and possessions, looking at every reference to this subject in every part of the Bible. Very thorough and not for the casual reader, but it is worth a look if you want to think more on this subject.

Mark Lloydbottom – *Your Money Counts* (Bristol: Crown Financial Ministries, 2008)
Mark Lloydbottom brings a lifetime of financial advising to this book. A worthy read for practical wisdom.

Tony Payne – *Cash Values: Money* (Sydney: Matthias Media, 2003)
Five short studies through various texts of the Bible to help you get further oriented to God's attitude to money. A great first resource to use in helping others to start thinking about money.

Keith Tondeur – *Your Money and Your Life* **(London: Triangle/SPCK, 2003)**

Though I have taken a slightly different approach, I found Tondeur to be really helpful. There were some insights that I would have liked to include, had space allowed, as he brings great experience of helping others (through Credit Action), and, thus, accumulated wisdom, to this book.

www.creditaction.org.uk

A great resource for information, statistics and advice on a range of topics, though majoring on debt. If you want debt advice, contact them on 0207 380 3390 or office@creditaction.org.uk

www.barnabasfund.org

Once you have your finances in some sort of order, why not aim to direct some of your giving, either individually or as a church, towards caring for the persecuted church around the world? God guarantees to honour such giving.

NOTES

Introduction
1. Matthew 5:14.

Chapter 1: Where it all started and how it all went wrong
1. www.statistics.gov.uk/cci/nugget.asp?id=1005. The figures are much higher (about 100%) for the very wealthiest and lower (about 10%) for the poorest. But, regardless of where you are on the scale, disposable income has risen consistently for those forty years.
2. www.statistics.gov.uk/STATBASE/ssdataset.asp?vlnk=6053.
3. Mark Lloydbottom (with Howard Dayton), *Your Money Counts* (Bristol: Crown Financial Ministries, 2008), p. 58.
4. Randy Alcorn, *Money, Possessions and Eternity* (Wheaton, IL: Tyndale House Publishers, 2003 edition), p. 439.
5. Keith Tondeur, *Your Money and Your Life* (London: Triangle Publishing/SPCK, 2003), p. 59.
6. Lloydbottom, ibid., p. 57.
7. According to the Office of National Statistics, the number of children per family has shrunk from 2.0 (1971) to 1.8 (2004) children per family (www.statistics.gov.uk/cci/nugget.asp?id=1163).
8. At least in the form of retail purchases. In practice the money would be loaned by banks for capital investment and research or lent internationally, but it would still affect domestic retail sales.

9. James W. Sire, *Naming the Elephant: Worldview as a Concept* (Downers Grove, IL: IVP, 2004), p. 122.
10. Craig L. Blomberg, *Neither Poverty Nor Riches* (Nottingham: IVP: Apollos, 2003 edition), p. 239.

Chapter 2: Who wants to live forever?

1. Song by Brian May, from the Queen album *A Kind of Magic* (1986).
2. www.newworldencyclopedia.org/entry/ John_D._Rockefeller (accessed 22 February 2010).
3. Randy Alcorn, *Money, Possessions and Eternity* (Tyndale House, 2003), p. 103.
4. Ibid., p. 78.
5. Ibid., p. 11.
6. Ibid., p. 19.

Chapter 3: What is your life worth?

1. Alcorn, ibid., p. 10.
2. Lloydbottom, ibid., p. 31.
3. Blomberg, ibid., p. 184.

Chapter 4: God's priorities for your money

1. Blomberg, ibid., p. 18.
2. Commenting on verse 8, Blomberg says: 'This verse says nothing about a man being the primary "breadwinner" for a family; the language is completely generic in the Greek. Instead, it says everything about working age adults, explicitly including women . . . having the responsibility to care for their elderly relatives. In the modern world, this of course does not dictate exactly how that care should be provided . . . but it does suggest that a family has financial responsibility to its own members before the church (or any other community)

should be burdened. This indeed was an ideal throughout antiquity. How disgraceful, therefore, if Christians behaved worse than the pagans among whom they lived (hence the language of verse 8b)', ibid., p. 208.
3. Lloydbottom, ibid., p. 35.
4. Tondeur, ibid., p. 85.
5. Blomberg, ibid., p. 162.
6. Ibid., p. 165.
7. Alcorn, ibid., p. 206.

Chapter 6: Where are you now?
1. The figures I am using come from the USA as I have been unable to locate similar research into UK church giving.
2. Blomberg, ibid., p. 20.
3. Alcorn, ibid., p. 209.
4. Ibid., p. 197.
5. Alcorn makes a good argument that our taxes are used for our benefit (e.g. in providing emergency services) and, therefore, the appropriate income to give from is your gross.
6. Ibid., p. 276.
7. www.statistics.gov.uk/pdfdir/ashe1108.pdf (accessed April 2008).

Chapter 7: Investing in your future
1. There are more variables here – the choice, for example, to work part-time and study part-time, or to live at home to save costs, to choose a cheaper course to study and so forth.

Chapter 9: Equipping the church
1. Tondeur, ibid., p. 127.
2. Alcorn, ibid., p. 399 – this is an excellent chapter in an insightful, if long, book.

Chapter 11: 'Excel in this act of grace also'
1. Blomberg, ibid., p. 132.

Chapter 12: Give as good as you get
1. It is likely that other First World governments operate similar systems.
2. To get this whole amount back, it should be noted, a self-assessment tax return is required.

Chapter 13: Making the most of your death
1. It is possible to give to charity out of an estate free from inheritance tax, but the benefit of this may be lost once the inheritance is received by a third party. It is best for the donor to give the gift free of tax through their will.
2. www.statistics.gov.uk/CCI/nugget.asp?ID=1105&Pos=6& ColRank=2&Rank=224 (accessed 22 February 2010).

Chapter 14: Radical church
1. Alcorn, ibid., p. 294.
2. Ibid., p. 105.
3. Ibid., p. 178.
4. Blomberg, ibid., p. 20.
5. Alcorn, ibid., p. 298f., taken from Charles Edward White 'Four lessons on money from one of the world's richest preachers', *Christian History* 19 (Summer 1988): 24.
6. Blomberg, ibid., p. 250f.
7. As quoted in *The Christian Pioneer* (1856) edited by Joseph Foulkes Winks, p. 84.
8. Alcorn, ibid., p. 422.

www.ivpbooks.com

For more details of books published by IVP, visit our website where you will find all the latest information, including:

Book extracts   Downloads
Author interviews   Online bookshop
Reviews   Christian bookshop finder

You can also sign up for our regular email newsletters, which are tailored to your particular interests, and tell others what you think about this book by posting a review.

We publish a wide range of books on various subjects including:

Christian living   Small-group resources
Key reference works   Topical issues
Bible commentary series   Theological studies

                    www.ivpbooks.com